BEYOND HETEROSEXISM
in the PULPIT

Beyond Heterosexism in the
P U L P I T

Emily Askew
O. Wesley Allen Jr.

WITH A FOREWORD BY
David Buttrick

CASCADE *Books* · Eugene, Oregon

Cascade Books
An Imprint of Wipf and Stock Publishers
199 W. 8th Ave., Suite 3
Eugene, OR 97401

www.wipfandstock.com

ISBN 13: 978-1-4982-2204-4

Cataloging-in-Publication data:

Askew, Emily, and O. Wesley Allen Jr.

    Beyond heterosexism in the pulpit / Emily Askew and O. Wesley Allen Jr.

    xii + 150 p.; 23 cm—Includes bibliographical references.

    ISBN 13: 978-1-4982-2204-4

    1. Homosexuality—Religious aspects—Christianity. 2. Preaching. 3. Heterosexism. I. Title.

BR115.H6 A80 2015

Manufactured in the USA.

For our spouses,
Viki and Bonnie,
with love.

Table of Contents

Foreword

THE TWENTIETH CENTURY BEGAN a huge linguistic revolution. In 1934, the unabridged *Webster's Dictionary* contained roughly 450,000 words. By 1960, we had lost at least a third of the words, but at the same time a new language was forming. Many of the new words were added from the hard sciences, many more from social sciences, and still more from a growing technology—television and computers. A book on new computer terms was published in the early 1960s, but now—more than two decades into the twenty-first century—most of those terms have faded and been replaced with a whole new terminology. High-tech words are still multiplying as preteens wander among us with cell phones on their ears, and then fix on the Internet when they are at home. They text their friends, and texting has now added a code list larger than LOL and OMG.

But there's another group of new words, wonderful new vocabulary brought about through difficult struggles for freedom and equality. Many of us can recall how hard it was for the feminist movement to gain recognition by men who were privileged by the patriarchal status quo. In one theological seminary, female students would rise up and stand in silent protest whenever a professor used a sexist phrase. In another school, women felt forced to blow police whistles to get professors to acknowledge their need for just language. While the struggle against sexism continues, such efforts produced much fruit. Our language has been forever altered. We can no longer comfortably say, "God, he." Churches have felt called to erase the sexist forms from our liturgies, our translations of the Bible, and our ecclesial conversations. And, indeed, now seminaries have many more female students in training for the ministry, and women are serving the church in pulpits and positions once reserved for men only.

Similarly, the civil rights movement used many strategies to bring about racial justice and equality, including an intentional shift in the way we use racially loaded language. On December 1, 1955, in Montgomery, Alabama, Rosa Parks refused to move to the back of a bus and yield her seat to a white rider. Suddenly the civil rights movement began in America. A young minister in Park's city of Montgomery named Martin Luther King Jr. stepped into leadership. Remember the dramatic Selma march that filled television screens everywhere. There were sit-ins and school integrations, and college students all over America became involved. While the struggle against racism continues, such efforts produced much fruit: our language has been altered radically. The "n-word" and the practice of calling adult men "boy" were banished. African Americans began to take control of naming themselves individually and as a community, and African American idiomatic language became part of cross-cultural American speech. R&B music from Detroit and rap music from both coasts has been enjoyed across racial lines. And now America has its first black president, something Rosa Parks probably couldn't have imagined in 1955.

Both of these social liberation movements have been aided by preachers speaking out prophetically and in solidarity with those who have come asking a share of the equality promised in our nation's Declaration of Independence. We should not diminish the power of pulpit speech to support and hasten freedoms for those who have been suppressed. At first speaking out in support of free equality may take courage and deliberate adjustment. Think of brave ministers who spoke out in support of Martin Luther King Jr. while serving somewhat conservative Southern congregations. Think of clergy ridiculed for supporting equal rights for women, as well as conversational respect for outspoken feminists.

Now we need to be using the pulpit to advance the liberation of another oppressed group, the gay community. Preachers can help change the language of the church's proclamation and rituals to support and interpret this need for freedom from heterosexism. You hold in your hands a book that's going to help you learn how to modify your language in order to welcome a new liberation with your preaching as well as your personal conversation.

The book has been cowritten by two distinguished faculty members from Lexington Theological Seminary: Dr. Emily Askew, professor of systematic theology, and Dr. O. Wesley Allen Jr., professor of homiletics and worship. They are nationally known and respected scholars. Teamed together, they can help you understand all that may be involved in altering your language and adding new terminology as the gay, lesbian, and bisexual community rises to new heights of public awareness and acceptance. This is no longer a "don't ask, don't tell" world. A Supreme Court decision has urged equal rights for homosexual individuals and couples. Ministers are called to speak with sensitivity and prophetic courage on behalf of the members of their congregations and communities who are gay.

So here's the book to teach us all how to be leaders in still another liberating movement. Ministry is a talking profession, and as we respond to the call to modify and enlarge our speaking, Askew and Allen help us to understand and welcome an unacknowledged group within every parish and culture. Further, they help us think through the regular rituals of Christian worship—the Lord's Supper, baptism, marriage, and funeral rites—in relation to building a nonheterosexist church and world. Here these splendid scholars help us to adapt, consider, and express a welcoming sensitivity for still another social group that has long waited for God's liberation to be offered to them. I am honored to celebrate their work.

David G. Buttrick
The Drucilla More Buffington Professor of Homiletics and Liturgics, Emeritus, Vanderbilt University

Introduction

THERE HAS BEEN MUCH positive movement for homosexuals in recent years. Don't Ask, Don't Tell (DADT) has been dismantled and many positive moves have been made in the military to guarantee the rights of gay soldiers and their loved ones. The Defense of Marriage Act (DOMA) and California's Proposition 8 were both effectively struck down by the Supreme Court on the same day, allowing same-sex couples to marry in California and forcing the federal government to grant financial and property rights to same-sex couples married anywhere. Poll after poll shows that the American public has shifted incredibly over the last two decades toward thinking gay men and lesbians should have the right to marry. And in the church more denominations and congregations have moved to accept gay members, perform same-sex weddings, and ordain gay leaders.

So perhaps this book is showing up to the party a little too late. We would counter, however, that while we thankfully hear fewer stories in the news of horrific homophobic violence—the sort of which Matthew Shepard was a victim—prejudice and discrimination against gay individuals and couples is still dancing the night away. In the same way that we no longer have lynchings of African Americans but racism is still around, and we no longer consider women the property of their husbands but patriarchy is alive and well, so biased attitudes and actions against homosexuals continue in more subtle and nuanced forms. Recently, in an interview concerning Uganda's law criminalizing homosexuality, an evangelical "pro-family" activist who has argued for the need for such laws tried to appear more moderate at the end of the conversation. He said,

> I believe that societies of the world have an affirmative duty to protect the natural family and to discourage all sex outside of marriage. And I'm talking about adultery, fornication, homosexuality,

1

incest, all of it. But I also believe that in our societies we should have, you know, reasonable tolerance for people who decide to live outside the mainstream discreetly. I think we had a pretty good balance in the 1940s and '50s in this country. Unquestionably, it was a family-centered mainstream culture and [there were] sub-cultures in which homosexuals and others could live out their lives and be happy. I love gay people. I wish they weren't doing what they were doing. And I don't want them to be harmed or hurt. I've never preached hatred or violence against them. I'd rather that they stop trying to mainstream this sort of anything-goes sexuality and, you know, go back to the original goal of seeking tolerance, the right to be left alone.[1]

The attitude seems to be that as long as gays are neither seen nor heard and don't expect to be acknowledged as human beings, they should be left alone. But should they peek out of the closet, they're fair game.

One might still argue that most biased attitudes and actions toward homosexuals in society, and certainly in our churches, are not as blatantly offensive and ugly as this opinion. But kinder and gentler forms of hatred are still hatred and an abomination to the Christian gospel. This book is intended to help pastors address the persistent forms of prejudice and discrimination against gays in society and in the church that will likely not disappear any time soon.

That means this is not a book trying to persuade the reader that homosexuality is not a sin, or reinterpret the scriptural passages that are thrown around in the debate concerning homosexuality, or argue that gays deserve the same civil rights (including the right to marry) that straight people possess, or push for the ordination of lesbians and gay men by the church. There are already numerous books that do these things well. More-over, we assume a pastor picking up this book is already on the progressive side of these sorts of issues.

Specifically, we are writing for pastors who feel called to speak prophetically on these issues while being pastoral to those in the pews who may not agree with her or his stance. Biased attitudes in the pews can lead a preacher either to avoid issues related to sexual orientation out of fear of rejection from the congregation or to rail against the issues in ways that

---

1. Scott Lively interviewed by Michel Martin on *Tell Me More* from NPR News: "Uganda Punishing Gays: 'Sodomy is Not a Human Right' Says Evangelical Leader," http://www.npr.org/2014/02/27/283456094/uganda-punishing-gays-sodomy-is-not -a-human-right-says-evangelical-leader.

alienate hearers instead of inviting them to have a change of mind, heart, and behavior. Of course, the picture is more complex than this. Rarely is a congregation of one mind. How do we preach about these issues so that gay members feel affirmed, cared for, and protected by the church without shaming straight members to the point of resistance or inaction? How do we address the range of informed and uninformed attitudes concerning homosexuality held by various heterosexuals in the congregation?

In the pages that follow, we strive to offer preachers theological and ethical language along with homiletical strategies to inform preaching that addresses prejudice and discrimination aimed at homosexuals, but which offers God's good news to everyone in the pews at the same time.

THE SCOPE OF THE BOOK

Preachers must find ways to address issues related to LGBTQI (Lesbian, Gay, Bisexual, Transexual/Transgender, Queer/Questioning, Inquiring/Intersex) persons. The full complex of issues related to sexual orientation *and* gender identity are beyond the scope of this book. Even though the issues across this spectrum of individuals and groups are similar enough to warrant joining together in terms of advocacy, they have enough differences and distinct nuances that we risk being reductionist by trying to deal with them all in a book of this sort. We have chosen, therefore, to focus narrowly on addressing from the pulpit the issues of prejudice and discrimination against homosexuals. We do hope, however, that some of the suggestions made in the pages that follow suggest analogous theological and homiletical language and strategies for addressing related issues.

In addition to the topic itself requiring focus on biased attitudes and actions against gay persons, the focus of the book reflects the expertise the two of us bring to the range of issues affecting the LGBTQI communities. Emily Askew and Wes Allen are colleagues and friends who teach together at Lexington Theological Seminary. In terms of sexual orientation, Emily is a lesbian who has felt the sting of prejudice and discrimination, and Wes is a straight ally who has experienced the privilege that accompanies being a Euro-American, heterosexual, middle-class male. In professional terms, Emily is a theologian and Wes is a homiletician. In relation to sermons, Emily is a lay listener, and Wes is an ordained preacher. In denominational terms, Emily is a member of the Christian Church (Disciples of Christ), which recently passed a resolution affirming homosexuals as church members and clergy, and Wes is a member of the United Methodist Church, which continues to debate the issue of homosexuality but holds as official church law that homosexual behavior is incompatible with Christian teaching. The range of experiences, knowledge, and skills we have brought to the project make this a very different (and we think, better) book than if either of us had written it alone.

As noted above, the type of bias in moderate to progressive "mainline" sorts of churches that preachers need to address these days and in the coming days is less likely to be blatant homophobia (although we are under no illusion that verbal and physical gay bashing will cease to continue to play a role in our society) and more likely to be more subtle forms of discrimination. To be explicit, by "homophobia" we mean fear-inspired and hateful acts of bigotry toward gays. Although at times used as a synonym for homophobia, "heterosexism" better describes a broader category of which homophobia is a particular expression.

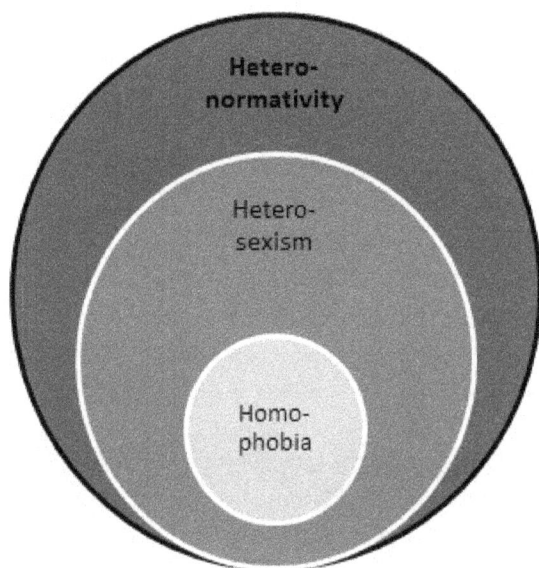

Heterosexism includes all forms of sexual prejudicial attitudes, actions, and structures that contribute to personal, institutional, and societal discrimination of LGBTQI individuals and the LGBTQI community as a whole. Heterosexism is possible because of "heteronormativity," the explicit or implicit and pervasive assumption by individuals and societies that heterosexuality is the norm for biological sex, gender identity, sexual orientation, and sexual relationships. Most "mainline" churches and denominations exhibit little outright homophobic behavior or attitudes these days, but most—even those that are "open and affirming" toward homosexuals—hold on (often unconsciously) to heteronormative world views and the privilege that they grant to heterosexuals in culture and the church, thus allowing (or even perpetrating) heterosexism to manifest itself in the way individual Christians and the community of faith speak and act. Thus, heteronormativity and heterosexism are the primary forms of bias with which most preachers will be confronted and with which, therefore, this book deals.

THE STRUCTURE OF THE BOOK

There are three main liturgical occasions in which preachers will have opportunity to address issues of heterosexism. The first is the pattern of preaching in regular worship week in and week out. In other words, when preachers who follow the Revised Common Lectionary or develop topical sermon series are not addressing heterosexism directly as the main focus of the sermon, they should still have an eye toward avoiding and countering heteronormativity and heterosexism as an element of the sermon. One of the ways to do this is to re-vision the way we conceptualize and communicate key doctrines of the faith that have played a role in bias against homosexuals. We start the book with two case studies of this sort. In Chapter 1 we examine the matrix of doctrines dealing with theological anthropology, sin, and soteriology. In Chapter 2 we offer a nonheterosexist approach to ecclesiology.

The second liturgical occasion in which preachers might address heterosexism is when a specific issue of gay rights or specific incident of discrimination against a gay person or group has come to light. The public nature of the issue or incident serves as a calling to the preacher to speak out of a sense of justice. At these times, the issue may indeed become one of homophobia, but it need not be at that level of hateful fear to call for an immediate and direct response. In Chapter 3 we deal with preaching related to these specific issues of gay rights.

The third liturgical occasion that we should use to preach in a way that invites hearers to move beyond heterosexism is at pastoral rites performed for homosexual individuals or couples. Chapter 4 deals with preaching at same-sex unions and weddings, and Chapter 5 with funerals and memorial services for gay persons.

Finally, the book concludes with a glossary of common, technical, and slang terms thrown around in discussions of gay issues without always being clearly defined. We include such a glossary as a way not only of clarifying meanings, but also of providing advice about the appropriateness of different terminology in the pulpit.

Each of the five chapters follows a similar fourfold structure in dealing with its particular focus. An opening scenario puts a face on the issue lifted up in the chapter. Then considerable length is given to a theoretical—that is, theological, ethical, liturgical, and/or cultural—discussion of the issue. Theory gives way to practical advice about preaching at the end of the chapter. Finally, a sample sermon is provided that exemplifies the approach (or elements of the approach) suggested in the chapter.

OVERARCHING HOMILETICAL STRATEGIES FOR MOVING BEYOND HETEROSEXISM

Throughout the material that follows, we will offer two types of homiletical strategies for dealing with the focus of the individual chapters. The first type consists of a set of longitudinal strategies for addressing the subject matter throughout one's preaching ministry, across the span of many sermons. The second type is that of narrower suggestions for dealing with the subject matter of the chapter in the context of a single sermon.

Here at the opening of the book, however, it is important to establish some strategies for moving beyond heterosexism in the pulpit that are more general than the topics in the chapters allow. These strategies serve as the foundation upon which all the other strategies offered in the chapters are built. Indeed, often the strategies in the chapters will be nuanced versions of a general strategy offered here.

Since not everyone in a congregation is in agreement about how the church should deal with homosexuals and approach the issue of heterosexism theologically, and since the church's debate about homosexuality has been and continues to be filled with highly charged rhetoric and emotions, we urge progressive pastors to find a homiletical voice with which they can be prophetic and pastoral at the same time. *Prophetic* in the sense of taking the risk of standing up courageously in the name of God for homosexuals who have been oppressed and thus in calling for justice in the church and society. *Pastoral* in the sense of having compassion in the name of God for oppressors who are trapped in the very heterosexist systems that accord them privilege, trapped in that they are cheated of the ability to love and experience love from neighbor and God fully. As we preach to homosexuals the good news of God's liberation from oppression, we must at the same time offer to heterosexuals good news of liberation from being oppressors. If those who have actively supported or unconsciously benefited from heteronormativity, heterosexism, and/or homophobia leave a sermon only feeling guilty, accused, or beaten up, they will have not been offered the hope and peace of the gospel of Jesus Christ that can inspire them to repent of the sins of heterosexism and live into a new reality where they are freed from their own prejudices. Our task in the pulpit is never simply to speak a prophetic word, but to speak it in a way that those who would initially rather not listen can hear it, embrace it, and live it out.

Walking the tightrope that is tied to prophecy at one end and pastoral care at the other is never an easy task, but it is especially difficult given the diversity of the congregations to which we preach. It would be much easier to preach this sermon to gay people who have been oppressed and that sermon to straight people who have never known discrimination on the basis of their sexual orientation, this sermon to straight people who oppose heterosexism and that sermon to straight people who consider homosexuality a sin. But when we preach, we preach to whoever shows up on a given Sunday. Preachers know the difficulty of preaching across the diversity of age, ethnicity, race, socioeconomic levels, educational backgrounds, and so on and so forth represented in worship each week. Add to the mix the intention to address the sensitive and complex issue of heterosexism, and the tightrope gets even more wobbly.

Part of walking this tightrope involves preachers shaping their homiletical language with the awareness that gay and straight listeners will experience sermons and sermonic elements dealing with heterosexism differently. Of course, this is the case for sermons that do not address heterosexism as well: sermons that assume or never question heteronormativity may just seem "normal" to straight people, but homosexuals may feel excluded when they are never named—or worse, when they are stereotyped. Conversely, when heterosexism is appropriately exposed, homosexuals in the pews will feel affirmed while heterosexuals may feel uncomfortable, guilty, resistant, or angry. Preachers need not try to control or manipulate every aspect of a congregation's emotional experience in relation to their sermons, but we do need to be aware of the general range of responses we want to invite from different parties in the pews and what may help or hinder those responses from coming to fruition.

Preachers pastorally inviting a response to a prophetic stance concerning heterosexism should think about the issue of homiletical quantity. We should avoid trying to tackle too much of heterosexism in a single sermon. This is true for dealing with any subject matter in the pulpit. No one can deal with the entirety of any social issue, much less preach the whole of the good news of Jesus Christ, in a single sermon. Likewise, heteronormativity has been around for millennia and will not simply disappear after a twenty-minute sermon. It runs through the pages of Scripture and church teaching like pollution pouring from an industrial complex into a small creek. And even with recent advances made in public attitudes and civil rights related to homosexual individuals and couples, heterosexism is a daily experience for many gay people in America. No single sermon—no matter how eloquently it is preached or how forcefully the gospel is brought to bear on the subject—can dismantle the powerful reality that is heterosexism.

So preachers must be patient with their congregations without allowing the conversation about heterosexism to become stagnant—patient, but neither tolerant nor silenced. Seasoned preachers know that while we hope and pray for the sermon that changes lives radically, it is preaching week in and week out to the same community of faith that has subtle, yet very real, transformative power. Instead of tackling the whole of heterosexism once in a sermon on National Coming Out Day in October, preachers will do better to work on tearing apart heterosexism a little bit at a time over the course of many sermons.

In other words, while there are times when preachers must be willing to name the injustice of heterosexism explicitly (for instance, in response to hate speech or physical violence against someone in the community), we must also become agile at helping the congregation move beyond heterosexism in more implicit and evocative ways when sermons are dealing with the whole range of topics that we are called to address across the span of the liturgical year and in leading the congregation in all aspects of its faith journey. A significant element of countering heterosexism in the pulpit thus is simply normalizing the congregation's view and speech about gay persons and relationships. In other words, we must unmask the unhealthy and unjust constructs that divides communities and cultures on the basis of sexual orientation (without erasing all differences between people). In heteronormative circumstances, speaking of homosexuals, same-sex relationships, or issues important to the gay community is extra-ordinary, even if the community sees itself as accepting of gay people. Preachers should be as much at ease in speaking of a homosexual couple as they are of speaking of a heterosexual couple. When we speak of God's care for society, we should name heterosexism as easily and often as we name discrimination related to race, age, sex, class, religion, and ability.

One way to normalize homosexuality in our sermons is to use homiletical litanies that include gay people, use issues related to the lives of gay people, and use examples of heterosexism without solely focusing on it. For instance, in a sermon calling the church to move beyond its walls and care for the world, we might offer a list of social ills with heterosexism or homophobia included in the mix. Or in talking about baptism breaking down the walls of division within the church, we might expand upon Paul's list in Galatians 3:28: "There is no longer Jew or Greek, there is no longer slave or free, there is no longer male or female; no longer black or white; no longer gay or straight; no longer young or old, rich or poor, good-looking or ugly, abled or disabled; for all of us are one in Christ Jesus." When we use extended lists like this in our sermons, we do not intend our congregation to remember the items we name so much as we intend for the list as a whole to have an emotional impact on them. By placing the pairing of gay and straight in the middle of the list instead of at the beginning or end, homosexuals are included without being highlighted in a way the others listed are not.

Similarly, when we use a range of images in a sermon about something other than heterosexism, there is an opportunity to include an illustration that involves a gay person or couple. This can be especially helpful in normalizing homosexuality for the hearers when the use of a gay person or couple in the imagery has nothing to do with sexuality or sexual orientation: a lesbian who is a model of philanthropy, a gay couple caught in the web of materialism, an older gay man struggling with arthritis. In other words, we need to be at ease with speaking about and helping the congregation be at ease hearing about gay people simply as people. We need to use homosexual characters in stories with whom we want everyone in the pews (regardless of their sexual orientation) to identify. In sum, we need to use gay people in our sermons as representative humans instead of only as representative homosexuals.

A warning must accompany this suggestion. Preachers must avoid tokenizing or actually setting apart gay people in the very process of trying to normalize speech about them in a heteronormative culture and congregation. Consider, for example, a white man telling a story in which he refers to one of the characters in the story as a "black woman," although he does not name the race or ethnicity of anyone else in the story, and the race of the woman has no significance in the story at all. The storyteller may not have intended to discriminate against anyone on the basis of race, but he has nevertheless exposed the assumption that white is normative and black is "other," and to talk about a black person is extra-ordinary. If we start a story with, "I know a lesbian who is especially generous," we single her out as different than "normal" straight people and may even make her sound like an exception to some rule of stingy lesbians of which our congregation has never heard, instead of lifting her up as a person who is a model for the kind of charity to which we all aspire. In other words, such expressions actually deconstruct our very attempt to normalize gays in the world view of straight people in our congregation and can do more harm than good.

An example of being more subtle and inviting is illustrating the problems of materialism by first telling a story of Lisa and John buying so much "stuff" for their home that they struggle to pay their bills. We do not have to say the two are a couple or married because most people will assume such by the description of a shared home and shared bills. We can follow this with a story of Markus and Tom that has the same type of structure and similar details concerning a shared home and bills. Without naming them as a committed gay couple, the parallels have made it clear that this is the case, while our primary focus on materialism stays intact.

Placing issues related to heterosexism and homosexuals into the mix of language and imagery used in sermons that are not focused on heterosexism are important ways of normalizing homosexuality for a congregation and play an important role in dismantling heterosexism over the course of preaching week in and week out. But this strategy will only have weight and influence if, as we mentioned earlier, preachers also speak explicitly and directly against heterosexism from time to time. This raises the question about the best way to name heterosexism directly in order to invite the congregation to embrace a different way of viewing and being in the world than heteronormativity allows.

There are times in the life of a congregation when pastors should name explicitly an injustice we have seen perpetrated in the congregation against a gay person—the rejection of a gay boy in the youth group or hurtful language in the discussion of whether a lesbian can hold office in the congregation. But hopefully we will more often be able to address heterosexism in times when an immediate crisis has not arisen. In these cases, we will do best to cast the word "you" out of sermons and resist pointing fingers at our congregation. Human beings have strong defense instincts, and when someone holds a mirror directly in front of our face, we have the incredible ability to reinterpret and even deny what we see. Directly accusing the congregation of being heterosexist will probably push more straight people away than invite them into a new conversation and could make gay people in the congregation feel more isolated than supported.

At the very least, then, straight preachers need to use "I" and "we" instead of "you" in directly addressing heterosexism. When straight preachers admit the ways in which "I" have lived out the privileges accorded to heterosexuals in a heteronormative culture and ways "I" have mistakenly or unconsciously discriminated against the gay community or gay individuals, we invite members of the congregation who are straight to identify with us and open themselves to admitting "our" role in the sins of heterosexism.

In addition to this occasional approach, both straight and gay preachers will often need to use "they" in explicit naming of dismantling heterosexism. The "they" here is not those gay others over against us straight people. Instead, we simply mean that we should use heterosexist characters and communities in our imagery that are distinct from the heterosexist congregation to which we are speaking and of which we are a part. Using examples of heteronormativity and heterosexism outside the congregation and its immediate context does not create an illusion that our community of faith is free from such problems. On the contrary, it creates a safe distance between the characters in the story and the hearers that allows members of the congregation in turn to look at themselves more critically. When hearers are able to feel discomfort or even disdain at something outside their own lives or their own congregation, they can then move on their own to the desire to root it out from their own midst as well. In other words, when the preacher holds up a magnifying glass on "their" heterosexism instead of a mirror on the same thing inside the congregation, the congregation is actually given the chance to notice their own translucent reflection in the magnifying glass as they focus through the lens to the image presented by the preacher.

The "they" must not always be negative, however. Showing our hearers persons and communities outside of "ours" that have faced their heterosexism, overcome it, and struggled against structural forms of heterosexism help our hearers know that "we" can take the same path. As that starts happening in the congregation, the preacher can pull the "we" and even the "you" back out in celebration and praise of the work that has been done in dismantling heteronormativity and heterosexism.

Having noted above the different use of pronouns based on whether the preacher is gay or straight leads us to one final observation. As gay and straight parishioners experience sermons differently, so will a congregation (in all its diversity) experience sermons dealing with heterosexism differently depending on whether they are preached by a gay or straight preacher. This is understandable given that the former addresses the subject matter as a victim of heterosexism and the latter as one who has privilege due to the system of heteronormativity but strives to be an ally to the gay community. A straight preacher cannot speak existentially about what damage heterosexism does to people in the same way a gay preacher can. On the other hand, a straight preacher has a different sort of power to speak prophetically about heterosexism because he/she cannot be dismissed as simply arguing for his/her own rights (as if that should ever be seen as negative!).

Heterosexual preachers, as mentioned above, must be honest—with themselves and their congregations (without using the pulpit as a confessional)—about the privilege they have experienced due to heteronormativity in culture and in the church. If they cannot name their own participation in this structural sin, they cannot lead a congregation out of that sin or into the struggle against it. One of the ways of examining how this privilege has been lived out vocationally is to survey past sermons, looking for ways they have assumed and reinforced heteronormativity.

- How have I presented love, marriage, and sexuality implicitly as well as explicitly in heterosexual terms?

- How often have gay people been used in imagery to illustrate something other than being gay?

- Is the only time sexuality is mentioned in sermons in relation to homosexual issues (even if the stance is one against discrimination based on sexual orientation)?

- How have I presented myself in relation to people who are homosexual, fighting for rights for them or with them?

- Have I tokenized homosexuals in my sermons in order to make myself look more progressive on issues of gay rights?

Homosexual preachers, on the other hand, need to be aware of the way a congregation—particularly straight members of a congregation who assume and benefit from heteronormativity—will hear them differently than they would a straight preacher. These differences may not be fair, but they are realities that must be considered if the hearers are going to be invited to embrace the gospel in a way that rejects and struggles against heterosexism. Gay preachers may be heard as "only" grinding their own ax when they address heterosexism. One way to counter this is to combine discussion of and concerns about heterosexism with other "isms," as suggested above. Homiletical misery loves company, as it were. Another way, of course, is for gay preachers to be honest about and share with the congregation (again, without using the pulpit as therapy) ways they have experienced pain inflicted by heterosexism. Sharing appropriate parts of their story can help gay members of the congregation identify with the preacher and feel that their experiences have been named in the context of the gospel and can at the same time invite straight members of the congregation who have a relationship with the pastor to empathize and perhaps engender in them righteous indignation concerning heterosexism and homophobia.

On the other hand, gay pastors cannot assume that simply because the congregation hired them, listens to them preach each week, and loves them, they also agree that heterosexism is a social issue they need to address, much less recognize the way they continue to live out heteronormative approaches to life and community. They may think, "We have gay people in our church; we have a gay pastor; we've done all we needed to do." In fact, they may actually be insulted that they still have to listen to sermons on the subject of heterosexism. Gay preachers may still need to tread carefully.[2]

2. Olive Elaine Hinnet shares experiences of just such a dichotomy in her book *God Comes Out: A Queer Homiletic* (Cleveland: Pilgrim, 2007), 1–3, 133–34.

1

Anthropology and Soteriology

An engaged couple came to you for their final premarital counseling session in which they talked about the wedding service that would be used. The couple had requested a traditional service, but you pointed out how the father "giving away" the bride along with the promise to obey as part of the vows were demeaning to women and not the best way to characterize the marriage they had said they wanted to create in earlier counseling sessions. The couple agreed and modified the liturgy so that it was not sexist, and you were appropriately satisfied.

At the wedding, you proudly led the couple and their loved ones through the service piece by piece, beginning with the greeting:

> Friends, we are gathered together in the sight of God
>> to witness and bless the joining together of Joan and Markus
>> in Christian marriage.
> The covenant of marriage was established by God,
>> who created us male and female for each other.

At the reception after the service, the sister of the bride thanks you for all you have done for the couple, but then says, "Pastor, you may not know that I'm a lesbian. I love my sister and brother-in-law and want them to be as happy as humanly possible. So I would never miss being here at her wedding, even though it's a ritual that's not available to me and my partner. But I do wish that I didn't have to be told at every wedding that I attend that God created me only to be with a man. Is that what you really think?" At that point, you realize that even though you have been adamant that no wedding you perform be sexist, you had never even noticed the way the language of the ceremony characterized all of humankind as created by God to be heterosexual, and *only* heterosexual. What theology and language can you turn to to correct this problem?

THEOLOGICAL ANTHROPOLOGY

At its core heterosexism in the church and in the pulpit is sustained by constructions of theological anthropology—questions of the worth, dignity, and responsibilities of human beings to themselves, to one another, and to God. From interpretations of our created nature come interpretations of how and why we sin and thus why and how we are saved. Heterosexist answers to the questions of creation, sin, and salvation assume limited interpretations of human sexuality and relationality. In this section we re-vision heterosexist interpretations of the worth and purpose of human sexuality (in creation, sin, and salvation) in ways that focus on the *quality* of human/divine and human/human relationships rather than on the necessity of genital complementarity.

Heterosexist Anthropology: Spirit-Body Duality

Different from the rest of the natural world, the creation story in Genesis 1 tells us that humanity is made in God's image, and that God proclaimed us to be "very good." Traditional heteronormative interpretations of the subsequent creation story in Genesis 2 assume the *imago Dei* is unpacked in terms of two theological mandates: 1) God privileges male and female partnerships over any other sexual pairing; and 2) the purpose of sexuality for humans, as for all of nature, is procreation. From these two theological mandates comes the standard definition of what is "natural" for human sexual relationships, the standard against which all other sexual relationships are judged, that is, the union of one man and one woman for the purposes of producing children.

Even though theologically progressive preachers argue against interpretations of the biblical "clobber passages" used by others to claim that homosexuality is a sin,[1] we often unconsciously promote heteronormativity

1. It is often argued that the Bible has several direct condemnations of homosexual behavior (Lev 18:22; 20:13; Rom 1:27; 1 Cor 6:9; 1 Tim 1:10) as well as stories presenting homosexual behavior as sinful (Gen 19:1–11; Judg 19:16–24). See Chapter 2 for a

by assuming the paradigmatic validity of these interpretations of the opening chapters of Genesis. This granting of authority to the traditional reading may not seem to be the case, since contemporary Protestant thought has long abandoned procreation as the sole end of committed heterosexual sex.[2] This move, however, is due mainly to the socioethical concerns for either heterosexual couples who cannot have or do not want to have children or about the problem of overpopulation. It is not, however, a rejection of the definition of "natural" sexual relationships as requiring the *potential* to procreate. In other words, the purpose of heterosexual sex is called into question but not the normative nature of heterosexuality itself. The move is heteronormative in that it focuses solely on redefining *heterosexual* relationships and not at all on the acceptance of same-sex relationships as a blessed part of God's creation.[3] To re-vision the good of our creation without relying on unspoken heterosexist assumptions we have to remember that our human nature is imprinted with the image of God. The history of the ways we have defined of the *imago Dei* shows us that there are important real-world consequences to how we define our likeness to God, but also that there is an openness in interpretation that is both consistent with the Christian tradition and relevant to our striving to be faithful, just, and compassionate in our contemporary service to God. Such an approach to biblical interpretation, relying on both tradition and the movement of the Spirit, is a direct application of the Protestant principle *ecclesia reformata, semper reformanda* (the church reformed, always reforming). This acceptance of evolving interpretations opens a door for us to propose and preach a nonheterosexist approach to the *imago Dei*.

Any theological formulation of what is to be considered "natural" human sexuality must include an interpretation of the biblical claim that humans—all humans—are made in God's image as claimed in Genesis 1:26–28:

> Then God said, "Let us make humankind in our image, according to our likeness . . ." So God created humankind in his image, in the image of God he created them; male and female he created them. God blessed them, and God said to them, "Be fruitful and

---

discussion of ecclesiological approaches to these texts.

2. See the discussion of the purpose of marriage in Chapter 4.

3. This problem of assuming heteronormativity can also be found in some feminist readings of Genesis 1–3 and the doctrine of the *imago Dei*; e.g., see Phyllis Bird, "Genesis I–III as a Source for a Contemporary Theology of Sexuality," *Ex Auditu* 3 (1987), 31–44.

multiply, and fill the earth and subdue it and have dominion over
the fish of the sea and over the birds of the air and over every living
thing that moves upon the earth."[4]

In this text, the image of God imparted to humans is described in terms
of our having "dominion" over the earth and the other animals (see also
Psalm 8).[5] This hierarchical distinction between humans and the rest of the
animal world has been the key to Christian expansion of the interpretation
of the *imago Dei* in that theologians and philosophers have focused on ways
humans are created as part of the animal world and ways that they can be
distinguished from the rest of the animal world. For centuries, they have
interpreted the best of human creation to be our rational, spiritual natures
(from God) over against our physical natures (from animals). Indeed, humans are able to reason and make existential meaning in a fashion other
animals are not.

This interpretation of the *imago Dei*, however, has led to a dualism in
which the physical, material aspects of life are denigrated, which, in turn,
has been used to support patriarchy and misogyny. From ancient times
on, men have characterized women as being more body-oriented in life, as
seen in their physiological relation to reproduction (menstruation, gesta-
tion, childbearing, and lactation). Men have used this characterization to
look down on and subjugate women as being controlled by emotions and
physical forces. Men, on the other hand, who do not menstruate or give
birth, have characterized themselves as being more intellectual and spiritual and thus as manifesting a stronger image of the divine than women do.
The theological necessity of the male/female sexual pairing ensured that
bodily, women would be successfully managed by their rational fathers and
husbands in order that they not give over to their more mutable (and thus
less Godlike) natures. In short, this interpretation has assumed that God

---

4. For other references in the Hebrew Bible to humankind being made in the image/
likeness of God, see Genesis 5:1–2; 9:6; Psalm 8; see also Wisdom 2:23, and in the New
Testament, James 3:9.

5. Much exegetical and theological work has been done in recent years critiquing
the way this dominion has been understood in the past in terms of humans dominating
and using the world needs to be replaced with a sense of stewardship in which humans
are responsible for the care of the world that sustains us. This exploration is beyond the
limits of our focus, but the work done in such re-visioning is a model for the approach
we are proposing.

made man in God's image (through the breath breathed into Adam) and God made woman in man's image (through the use of Adam's rib).[6]

This elevation of the mind and the soul coupled with the denigration of the body has especially led to a view of sexuality as overflowing with the potential for sin. Sex is not interpreted as a reasoned encounter—it is bodily desire; it is physicality; it is dangerous. But it is also necessary for the propagation of humanity. Thus theologians have argued that the sexuality of fallen humanity has to be controlled by the moral forces of reason and spirit in order that it not remain or become "animalistic." This control was exerted in the form of restricting "appropriate" sex (i.e., sex that is not sinful) to the reasonable confines of heterosexual marriage that holds the potential for procreation.

It is easy to see how this interpretation of human nature in relation to the *imago Dei* supports heterosexism. There is no place at all in this theological construct for homosexual sex, even in a loving, committed, and healthy relationship. It cannot be viewed as a good of creation. If heterosexual materiality, and especially sexuality, eclipses God-given reason, how much more sinful is homosexuality, which can be characterized by this viewpoint as not only unreasoned but also "unnatural," i.e., as unable to produce offspring. The progression of the argument looks something like this:

1. Heterosexual sex within marriage is acceptable. It is natural because it can result in offspring and is morally appropriate because desires have been controlled.

2. Heterosexual sex outside of marriage is sinful. It is natural because it can result in offspring but is morally inappropriate because it has not been controlled.

3. Homosexual sex is terribly sinful. It is unnatural because it cannot result in offspring and is morally inappropriate because desires have not been controlled.

Thus one legacy of this traditional interpretation of the *imago Dei* and its resulting tension between the high valuation of reason and spirit and the perceived corruption of the physical is the unavoidable condemnation of homosexuality. Even though progressive Protestantism has cast aside procreation as *the* purpose of sexuality, the concept (at least in terms of the

---

6. This dichotomy is explicitly named by Paul in 1 Corinthians 11:7.

potential for reproduction) still plays a significant role as an unexplored subtext in our broader interpretation of the creation stories, the *imago Dei,* and "natural" human sexuality. The divine spark is safe only when human sexual practices are oriented toward procreation, or at the very least are performed in the context of a married (i.e., controlled) heterosexual union of one man and one woman where procreation is possible.

Nonheterosexist Anthropology: *Hesed*

Rethinking this interpretation of the *imago Dei* does not necessitate throwing out the baby of reason with the bathwater of heteronormativity. It does, however, require cleansing the baby of a hegemony rooted in an understanding of the human no longer tenable. In the ancient world, with its lack of any complex understanding of human physiology, differences between humans and other animals had to be explained in terms of a special gift God gave to humans alone (the God of the gaps approach is not a modern phenomenon!). But with the advances in evolutionary biology and neurology, these differences can be explained scientifically. We now know humans share most of our DNA with other animals. Popular thought immediately turns to primates, but we actually share about 97.5 percent of our genes with mice (which is why so much research targeted toward human needs is done on mice). We even share some 70 percent of our genes with sea sponges! At our core, we are more like the rest of the animal world than our prescientific forebears could have ever imagined.

Still, that 2.5 percent difference between us and mice is a genetic continental divide. Even though humans are made of the same stuff as our animal cousins, what we have achieved with that stuff as a species is beyond comparison with the basic, instinctual existence of other species. We can think abstractly; solve complex problems; use resources in new and varied ways; develop cultures and societies; make tools and technologies to advance progress; create visual and performance arts; communicate complicated ideas using complex language systems; and conceptualize the world in moral, ethical, and religious terms in ways other animal species cannot. And we can do so, in a word, because we have bigger brains than they do. On the path evolution has taken, the brains of *homo sapiens* have developed into much more powerful organs than the brains of other animals. Thus the traditional theological stance about the difference between humans and other animals is on the right track—we can reason and make meaning in ways chimpanzees, mice, and sponges cannot.

The stance is wrong, however, in using this difference to construct a dichotomy in human nature between mind and body. The brain is just as much a part of the body as the genitals, and thus reasoning and making meaning—abstract thought, problem solving, language, and ethics—is as much a physical, material activity as sex is. A human being is a psychosomatic unity, not a "real" mind or soul trapped in an "illusory" body. It is the human being as a psychosomatic unity—both thinking *and* sensual—who is "very good" in God's eyes.

Since God is not needed to *explain* the differences between humans and other animals, we must recognize that the *imago Dei* is not a literal "thing" imparted to humans but a metaphorical explanation of those differences. Metaphors by their very definition compare two very different things in order to help us see the first item in the comparison anew. In this case, the unique qualities of being human (over against our similarities to other animals on the planet) are compared to the very image of God. Of course, part of the power of metaphors, as any good preacher knows, is that they are evocative instead of explicit. And context makes an incredible difference in what a metaphor evokes. In the prescientific, patriarchal, post-Hellenistic context through the Enlightenment, the church interpreted the metaphor of God's image as evoking a glorification of human reason over against human physicality. But in a context where that dichotomy is rejected, the potential for new evocations is present in the metaphor.

Metaphors depend on knowledge of the referent. If one says, "Congregational leadership is a professional wrestling match," the speaker assumes her or his hearers know something of the drama, fakeness, and staged violence of wrestling in today's media and through that knowledge gain some new understanding of the struggles of church politics. Thus when the Hebrew Bible speaks of humans created in God's image, the authors assume the hearers/readers know something of God's character that humans represent.

Of course, God's divine character as one who is both transcendent and immanent is expansive, including complex and paradoxical attributes. Reason can certainly be argued to be an element of God's character as presented in the Hebrew Bible. If we examine the representation of God's character throughout the canon, however, it is not reason that we find *centrally* emphasized. Instead, God is consistently portrayed as the sovereign One in loving and faithful relationship with God's creation and especially with God's children (i.e., humankind as a whole or, more narrowly, Israel). This relational quality of God is narrated in tales of liberation and providential care, proclaimed by the prophets (in both declarations of judgment and salvation), and celebrated in the prayers of the Psalter (even in laments asking why God has yet to show divine care for the ones in need). It is illustrated in its strongest form in the passages where God initiates and makes covenant with God's people. And it is summed up in the repeated use of *hesed* (weakly translated as "loving-kindness" and analogous but not exactly synonymous with the Greek concept of *agape*) to describe God's attitude and approach to humanity.[7]

While saying that humans are created in God's likeness potentially evoked a range of divine attributes for the ancient Israelites, it is not unreasonable to assert that for them the image of God in humanity might well have focused on the potential for relationships characterized by *hesed*. After all, the Hebrew Bible also repeatedly applies this descriptor to the actions of humans and the prophets call their hearers to enact such loving-kindness.

The potential for relationships characterized by *hesed* distinguishes big-brained humans from smaller-brained animals in the same way reason does. Humans make meaning of connections we have with other humans. This can especially be seen in sexual relationships: animals mate and reproduce, but they do not make love.

Once we emphasize relational *hesed* as the metaphorical description of God's image that is imparted to humans, we are no longer bound to heteronormative ways of describing "natural," appropriate, non-sinful relationships. Sexual relationships appropriate to the image of God are not defined by genital complementarity but by *hesed*. While one might argue that heterosexual sex is what makes us most like other animals, that is not what makes us like God. Meaningful, loving relationships are what are natural to our big-brained, God-imaged species. Thus the issue of opposite-sex versus same-sex relationships as part of the created order is a moot point. If the relationship is intimate, caring, respectful, committed, etc., it flows from God's image. In terms of intimate, sexual relationships, then, both homosexual love and heterosexual love are blessed as "very good" by the

7. *Hesed* is a complex multivalent Hebrew term for God's infinite love, mercy, goodness, and loyalty, and the corresponding behavior in God's people. See Gordon R. Clark, *The Word* Hesed *in the Hebrew Bible* (Sheffield: JSOT, 1993) and Katharine Doob Sakenfeld, *The Meaning of* Hesed *in the Hebrew Bible: A New Inquiry* (Missoula, MT: Scholars, 1978).

God who extends to us divine *hesed* and offers us the potential of extending *hesed* to one another.

Heterosexists create an atmosphere of fear by claiming that a move such as the one we propose—opening the door to homosexual relationships as an appropriate expression of the *imago Dei*—creates a slippery slope in which "anything goes" in terms of sexual ethics.[8] This is a specious argument. Like our animal cousins, we are indeed base sexual beings. But as a species who has tasted the tree of knowledge of good and evil, we know that some sexual activity (like some types of any category of behavior) can be harmful. A sexual ethic rooted in God's gift of *hesed* means the utter well-being of the other must always be of great concern in relationships. A sexual act that does not involve consent, mutual respect, and some type of commitment to the other as a person deserving of loving-kindness distorts the likeness of the relational God imparted to each of us.

Sin

If *hesed* is the mark of the relational God in humans, now understood not as a warring mind over an excessive body but as a psychosomatic unity, then how we conceptualize and preach sin changes dramatically. Like the understanding of the *imago Dei* revised here, traditional interpretations of sin demonstrate both that there are important, real world consequences to how we define sin and that there is historical malleability on which we can rely to determine nonheterosexist interpretations of sin.

Sin is popularly viewed in relation to a set of *behaviors* blessed or forbidden by God (the "Thou shalts" and "Thou shalt nots"). What is missed in such an understanding is that the Christian tradition calls us to pay attention at least as much to what it is that gives us the potential to behave sinfully—what we metaphorically call "original sin" or "fallen human nature"—as it does to sinful behavior itself. How we conceptualize "original sin" impacts what behaviors we determine to be "sins." In heterosexist interpretations of sinfulness related to sexual behavior, a strong factor in conceptualizing sinfulness is having an appropriate sexual (heterosexual) partner with whom we engage appropriate (procreative) sexual practices. Heterosexist discussions of homosexuality, then, fail to take into

---

8. Heterosexists often argue provocatively but illogically that if Christian theology or society views homosexuality as acceptable, it will soon be forced to accept pedophilia or even bestiality.

consideration two related elements of sin. First, sin should be understood as a common human condition, separate from particular embodiment (e.g., skin color, gender, sexual orientation). Second, this universality of sinfulness results not only in individual sinful behaviors but in the historical accumulation of those sins into structures of sin (e.g., racism, classicism, sexism, homophobia/heterosexism). By reincorporating the metaphor of original sin as a common human condition into a larger conversation about God's *hesed* as the mark of created difference from the rest of nature, we recognize that homosexuals are no more or no less sinful because of their sexual orientation than heterosexuals and are returned to both common blessedness and common sinfulness.

As a common human condition, original sin has been traditionally understood as the capacity to act against the good of others and the sovereignty of God. If the image of God in all of us is the potential for *hesed*, then sin is the condition in which we ignore, suppress, deny, or defy that potential. It is the failure to love God with our whole being and to love our neighbor as ourselves. We fail to love God and neighbor when we idealize the self—privileging *my* individual identity, needs, and desires over the identities, needs, and desires of others and our humility before God. In paying attention to *sin* rather than *sins* in this manner, practicing homosexuality is not inherently sinful, but homophobia as the oppression of gay people is.

Homosexuality per se is not a rejection of God's gift of *hesed*, but the structural sins of heterosexism and homophobia are. While people in the pews may usually think of sin as acts by individuals, systemic sin causes much more destruction towards many more people. Structural sin is the institutionalization of collective selfishness into a thoroughgoing cultural bias. One people take power over another. And in an evil, ironic twist, the hatred that goes against God's *hesed* in discriminating against gays (heterosexism and homophobia) turns the oppressed into deviants and thus "deserving" of whatever social/legal/theological punishment they get.

This twist of circular reasoning is, of course, nothing new. Structural sins manifested as sexism and racism identify the embodiment and sexual nature of certain groups (women and African Americans) as deviant and thus sinful. When a group is socially and politically oppressed, the oppression is legitimated by arguments appealing to their "sinfulness." Supposed sexual sinfulness especially justifies further social/political oppression. Above, we discussed the ways women have been cast as being more bodily/

physical (and so more sexual) than men and thus created less in the image of God, having more potential for sin than men and in need of the tempering effects of fathers and husbands. Similarly, African Americans have been cast as deviant "others" by the white majority. The treatment of African Americans under the gaze of racism serves as an analogy for what has happened to homosexuals under heterosexism and homophobia.

After white Christians enslaved Africans, they justified the enslavement by claiming that the slaves were dangerous to whites. Africans were described as being closer to animals than humans, and a significant part of that characterization involved describing male slaves as hypersexual with desires to rape or kill white women. Thus the "soulless" African slave was said to benefit from the "humanizing," indeed Christianizing, treatment and control they received by their white owners. Oppression of others different than "us" is followed by theological denigration of the others that includes the view that they lack sexual morals, which in turn justifies and invites more oppression.

Even 150 years after the ratification of the Thirteenth Amendment to the Constitution, which abolished slavery, African Americans still suffer under dominant culture's fascination with black men as sexually (and thus sinfully) dangerous. This perceived danger is often expressed in continued assumptions about the sexual proclivities of African Americans, the size of African American male sex organs, and the inappropriateness of interracial relationships. Thus the sin of racism continues to impact our treatment of African Americans, long after we have set some legal equality in place. It is odd indeed that systemic oppression is so successful in keeping some groups of people categorized as perpetual sinners simply by virtue of their status as "other," when the will to oppress and the act of oppressing others itself is a distortion of the *imago Dei* in us all. Oppressing others is a systemic violation of the principle and promise of *hesed*.

The homosexual community has certainly experienced this cycle of theologized oppression. The heterosexist powers that be reject them as different. That difference gets described in terms of "unnatural" sexual orientation and behavior that is sinful and dangerous to heterosexuals (for instance, in the claim that gay people want to "convert" heterosexual children into homosexuals). This theological rationale in turn has allowed, even promoted, gay bashing of all types to be acceptable to the point making gay relationships and behaviors illegal and prosecutable while majority infringement on the rights of gays as human beings continue (see Chapter 3).

While we progressive preachers certainly reject such overt oppression of homosexuals, we may unintentionally continue to legitimate heteronormativity and heterosexism (and even homophobia) by the ways we discuss sin in the pulpit. If we continue to speak of sin as acts performed by individuals instead of as a condition we share with all humans, we allow our heterosexual hearers to feel justified in looking down on same-sex orientation and behaviors as sinful. But it is our shared condition, with our individual predisposition to selfishness, that ends up in particular forms of collective selfishness as structural sin. The persistence of structural sin, in this case as institutionalized heterosexism, *indicts* those in the dominant culture who do not challenge the oppressive superstructures. If we speak of sins as a list of do's and don'ts, any challenge we make against heterosexism is weakened because hearers may agree with our characterization of sin but *disagree* with our particular list of what is to be considered sinful and what is not. Instead, if we consistently speak of sin as a capacity to deny and struggle against *hesed*, we are in a much stronger position to name how that sin is manifested and how it is not. From the standpoint of reflective, committed, mutual relating—the form of relationship we advance here as the true mark of what makes us like God—both heterosexual and homosexual relationships have the same capacities to be selfish or supportive. Homosexual relationships cease being sinful purely on the basis of same-sex desire, and heterosexual relationships cease being theologically ordained simply on the basis of other-sex desire and the potential for procreation. On the level of structural sin, the social superstructures that fail to treat entire groups of people with *hesed* can easily be seen as sinful.

A second change that comes when we re-vision sin away from behaviors and toward the quality of relationships between individuals and groups is that homosexuals are considered to share the human condition of sinfulness with the whole of humanity. Often progressive preachers, in a well-intentioned desire to remove the special stigma society and the church has leveled against gay men and lesbians, remove gays completely from descriptions of the common human condition. Sin is a condition of all humans. Thus homosexuals are sinners, not by virtue of being gay but by virtue of being human. Like all people, homosexuals distort our created good and damage the worth and dignity of others. Like all people, homosexuals ignore, suppress, and deny the God-imaged and God-given potential of *hesed*. Like all people, homosexuals fail to love God with our whole being and our neighbor as ourselves. Like all people, homosexuals idealize the self—privileging *my* individual identity, needs, and desires over the identities, needs, and desires of others. Like all humans, gay individual sin merges into structural sin, even advancing some forms of homophobia (see "Internalized Homophobia" in the glossary).

Homosexuals and homosexual relationships must be held to the same expectations of right relationship that the ethical standard of *hesed* calls all human beings to. Just as *hesed* shapes appropriate life-giving heterosexual relationships so that not "anything goes" simply because straight couples enact it, so homosexual relationships are equally shaped. Evaluating *all* intimate relationships in terms of loving-kindness, commitment, mutuality, respect, compassion, and the like undermines the homophobic argument discussed above that if homosexual relationships are given the same social, legal, and theological status as heterosexual relationships have, we will have started down the "slippery slope" to honoring any form of relationship.

A sexual ethic rooted in God's gift of *hesed* means the utter well-being of the other must always be of great concern in relationships. Sexual expression that does not involve consent, mutual respect, and some type of commitment to the other as a person deserving of loving-kindness distorts the likeness of the relational God imparted to each of us. In moving the emphasis in the discussion of sin from a list of behaviors to our common human condition, preachers name sin in sermons in a way that straight people recognize their own sinfulness instead of only seeing others as sinful and gay people recognize their sinfulness as unrelated to their homosexuality as such. The "fall" from our common human creation, a creation that God marks with God's own loving-kindness, to the selfishness of our common human sinfulness, individual and structural, requires that in God's saving grace we are restored to right relationship with God and with neighbor.

Salvation

Right relationship in the light of *hesed* means that our relationships are characterized by mutuality, compassion, and commitment, that is, by living out the goodness of being created human in the image of God. The action of being restored to living rightly with God and with one another is traditionally understood in the language of salvation—the unmerited gift of new life through the birth, life, death, and resurrection of Jesus Christ.

To begin our nonheterosexist re-vision of salvation, we must first recognize that while many progressive preachers believe fervently that being a homosexual does not merit God's one-way ticket to hell, we shy away from preaching salvation at all because we do not necessarily want to or know how to find a different theological way through traditional soteriological images and implications that confound our contemporary sensibilities and concerns. However, when we do not preach some kind of clear, consistent, and hopeful message of salvation, we unintentionally perpetuate the very theologies that we reject. Homosexuals need to hear a positive new word about God's salvific actions toward all people and not simply find in our sermons the absence of punishment for homosexuality.

Gay church members need this new word in order to crowd out the punitive soteriologies they have likely internalized since childhood. These internalized, sexually punitive theologies of salvation have written them out of God's grace unless they could "pray the gay away" before they died. In addition, heterosexuals need to hear a word that helps them overcome the shame and guilt they feel when faced with their unintentional complicity in sustaining a heterosexist and homophobic culture.

For all in the pews, this new word preached must be formed from and rely on the central soteriological symbols and questions in order to serve as a credible alternative for Christian hearers. As with the topics of creation and sin discussed above, we are not proposing an exhaustive soteriology in what follows, but rather we are offering a soteriological perspective that suggests ways that God's *hesed* is mediated to us through the person and work of Christ, in order to lay out the possibilities for creating and sustaining a different way of being together for the future. In doing so, we will focus on two topoi in terms of thinking about a nonheterosexist message of salvation: the meaning of the Christ event and the eschatological reign of God.

The Christ Event. To say that God became incarnate in the world in Jesus Christ is to say that we find in the story of the Christ event the clearest representation for Christians of God's loving-kindness from which and for which we are created. Trapped by our own human selfishness ("original sin"), we fail repeatedly to see for ourselves and by ourselves how fully and deeply we are loved by God and from that how we are compelled to love one another. God's revelation in the person and works of Jesus Christ proclaims in stark terms how far away we are from living out these values.

The depth of Jesus' commitment to work for others in the name of peace and justice is demonstrated by his death; his belief in being-with-others permeated to the very root of his life. He was not only for others, working on behalf of the vulnerable, but finally chose the condition of the other as his own. He chose to remain weak, in worldly terms, by refusing to condone violence as strength and demonstrating the depth of his convictions in his death. In his refusal to live by the power of the world (that is, death), the cross of Christ comes to describe the living the inversion of values we call the ethics of the reign of God. The cross gives us the measure of both our own sinfulness and our own convictions. To the extent that we say that the power of the cross endures, we acknowledge that every one of our relationships stands judged in the shadow of the cross. Each one of us is repeatedly given the opportunity to live differently. Mutuality rather than domination is the mark of the power of love. Mutuality is ultimately the power that not only transforms the individual in intimate relationships ,but, through individual transformation, moves toward breaking down the structural sins that oppress us and by which we oppress others.

A theology of living for others to the point of death with Christ as our model, however, has a long, unfortunate social history. Too many groups of people have suffered when sacrifice is demanded of those imprisoned by systemic sin—when victims of domestic violence are told that submission to the abuser makes them more Christlike, living out what God commands for women (misogyny and patriarchy); when African American slaves are told that suffering and death at the hands of slave owners is benevolent, an attempt to "Christianize" them (racism); when homosexuals endure repeated emotional and physical violence in forms of Christian reparative therapy (homophobia). In each of these cases, vulnerability is not equally distributed—it is forced on some to the benefit of others. Power over the other, rather than mutuality in relationships, is the basis for these sorts of calls to sacrifice. Thus sacrifice of those who are subjugated benefits those who do the subjugating. Power, however, cannot be relinquished by those who have none. Therefore calling for sacrifice from below is always oppressive. That said, while we pursue mutuality in intimate relationships and the conditions of thriving for all people, we recognize that vulnerability to the other will not look the same for each person in each relationship. Still, when *all* of us live our lives based on the cultivation of relationships of loving-kindness, and *all* of the privileged feel compelled to take on the vulnerable conditions of the powerless as their own, then we can say that a self-sacrifice as concern for the well-being of the other conforms to the likeness of Christ.

The Reign of God. As a consequence of Christ's ministry, death, and resurrection, those who followed Jesus chose this way of living together. Resurrection, as that which lives beyond Jesus' death, is/was the community of Jesus who persists in believing that caring for one another and creating relationships of justice, love, commitment, and healing is the steady stream that will ultimately dissolve the bedrock of entrenched systemic sin and the persistence of death-dealing relationships.[9] The community shaped by Christ attempts in our humble, painfully slow ways to live into and manifest what we believe to be the values of the reign of God. Confessing our sinfulness to one another before God, we are freed to create anew every day the conditions in which all of God's people can thrive—the conditions we believe to be from the very character of God.

Stated in terms of the focus of this book, then, salvation means that we are saved from perpetuating broken relationships and not from our sexual orientations. Resurrection is the transcendent value of loving-kindness that works with and through us in individual and communal relationships in the world, strengthened by our actions toward one another but ultimately outliving each one of us.

We must resist the easy triumphalism of relegating salvation to an otherworldly rescue of individual souls in favor of proclaiming salvation as this-worldly reconciliation involving a much more vulnerable dependence on one another. We are not saved from the world, but saved through the world, by virtue of the freedom to be the fullness of ourselves when others love us as equals and of the freedom we extend to others when we love in like manner.

It can be risky, though, to preach salvation as involving the transformation of relationships between individuals and systems in this world over against an otherworldly heaven and an extrahistorical eschatology. It is dangerous because even for progressive Christians, who believe that they have long ago given up heaven and hell as metaphorical, escape to another world where all suffering is at an end and one is reunited with lost loved ones is a deeply ingrained and powerful hope. Yet it is necessary because even though these forms of eschatological hope have kept marginalized

---

9. The idea of the mundane community as the place and form of resurrection is developed by a long line of theologians, but most recently and fully articulated in the work of Gordon Kaufman, *In Face of Mystery: A Constructive Theology* (Cambridge, MA: Harvard University Press, 1993).

communities physically and theologically alive in many respects, they have also too often been used to focus attention away from the work we have to do between ourselves in the here and now. Offering pie in the sky is never a suitable substitute for bread in the here and now.

We have to admit that humans do not have a great track record helping one another out, but if salvation is of God neither does the omnipotent, omniscient, and omnibenevolent God: questions of theodicy endure.[10] For us, salvific hope is Emmanuel, God *with* us as we work to live out the vision of life together expressed for us in Christ. Hope for the fulfillment of God's *hesed* then becomes a human practice, the exercise of a collective human muscle, strengthened every time we repent of our selfishness and repair the relationships we have broken in our particular sociohistorical setting. We exercise eschatological hope in the present with a vision toward the historical future and not a desire filled at the end of history.

In revising salvation as individuals and communities struggling to live out the *hesed* with which we are created, against which we often act and through which (by stories of Jesus Christ) we repair relationship, heterosexuals can be freed from the burdens of the guilt of being straight that people carry when struggling against a heterosexist culture. Likewise, homosexuals are freed to create full, God-blessed relationships without the constant shame of simply existing as gay persons. The good of our creation is our capacity to create life-giving, loving committed relationships with one another and to work for the conditions in which others can create the same kinds of relationships with one another. In this light, the relational ethics determine sexual ethics. How we relate to one another in intimate relationships and not the physiology of the ones to whom we relate determine our closeness or distance from the life God creates us for.

In our discussion of both human creation and sin here, we have moved our focus from heterosexuality, with its potential for procreation, to the quality of relationships we have with one another and with God as representative of our created good as well as our capacity for sin. Looking at the quality of our relationships rather than specifying embodiment lifts up some unexpressed heterosexism, and it serves to create a level theological playing field for gay and straight people. Our goodness and sin are judged equally based on the ways we care for the other. This leveling out extends all the way to salvation. In a soteriology based on the restoration of *hesed*,

10. Ivone Gebara, American Academy of Religion, Chicago, November 2012, plenary address.

"practicing" homosexuality is no longer a ticket to "hell." All are saved for right relationship.

HOMILETICAL STRATEGIES

Longitudinal Strategies

Helping a congregation deal with heterosexism in relation to the church's understanding of what it means to be human, to be sinful, and to be saved is no small homiletical challenge. These doctrines are the primary building blocks of Christian proclamation. While all arenas of Christian theology are important for proclamation, these are the ones that put the "good" and "new" into good news. The importance and complex nature of the doctrines individually, in relation to each other, and in relation to the vast landscape of the whole of systematic theology can be overwhelming and is certainly beyond the scope of this book.

As named above, however, *hesed* can serve as a handle for rethinking the three corralled doctrines that a congregation can easily grasp.

- Humans are made in the image of God in the sense that we share God's capacity for *hesed.*

- But we are sinful in that we reject the ethic of *hesed* given to us and act selfishly toward others for our own gain. This selfishness cannot be reduced to individual sinful acts—acting in ways counter to *hesed* is systemic in humanity and results in widespread discrimination, oppression, and violence.

- Yet God is true to God's character and responds to individual and systemic sin by offering God's *hesed* to the world, revealed paradigmatically in the person and works of Jesus Christ.

Preachers can repeat and rephrase this schema over and over again in sermons in diverse ways to counter clichéd approaches to sin as failing on the do's and don'ts and to salvation in terms of a substitutionary view of the cross. Indeed, changing the ways a congregation views human character in relation to the *imago Dei*, the human condition in relation to a systemic turning away from that image, and God's grace-filled response to our turning away helps a congregation move beyond heterosexism even without explicitly naming heterosexism in this context.

- Shaping our hearers' understanding of being made in God's image as having the capacity for *hesed* implies to them that all people, including homosexuals, are made in God's image.

- Shaping their understanding of sin as systemic failure to follow an ethic of God-given *hesed* implies that homosexuals are just as sinful as everyone else—i.e., not sinful *as* homosexuals, but sinful in the same way as everyone else. Moreover, this understanding also implies that homosexuals are victims of systemic non-*hesed* attitudes and sinful actions directed at them.

- Finally, shaping their understanding of salvation as God's *hesed* offered to liberate individuals and the world from sinful structures instead of a first-class ticket to heaven for certain individuals implies that salvation for homosexuals does not mean being converted to heterosexuality but being saved from heterosexism.

Thus, a primary longitudinal strategy for dealing with heterosexism in relation to theological anthropology and soteriology is simply proclaiming and interpreting these doctrines regularly in ways that do not implicitly exclude and do implicitly include homosexuals.

Implicit moves alone, however, will not be enough for congregations to make the explicit connections named above on their own. At times, across our preaching ministry, we need to explicitly relate these doctrines to heterosexism.

- We need to explicitly deconstruct the traditional interpretation of the creation of humankind in terms of gender complementarity and name that homosexuals are natural and created in God's *hesed*-image just as heterosexuals are.

- We need to explicitly present homosexuals (along with others we name explicitly) as victims of anti-*hesed*, sinful, structural oppression.

- And we need to explicitly proclaim God's gift of *hesed* as extended to homosexuals in light of heterosexism and homophobia.

Just as we deal with racism, sexism, classism, ageism, and the like in the pulpit, we have to explicitly deal with heterosexism in relation to these doctrines over and over again to have an impact on our congregation's theology and ethical/ecclesial behavior. Real change, even change that is a gift of God's *hesed*, is a slow process.

If we are to use *hesed* as an overarching theme of our preaching in a way that can have a positive effect countering heterosexism in the church, two issues need to be addressed. The first is one of vocabulary. When preachers use Hebrew or Greek words (or other technical language learned in seminary), the eyes of those in the pews can be found glazing over like icing dripping down over a cinnamon roll. Snoring is sure to follow soon. Terms like *hesed* have no connection to their vernacular and thus to their everyday reality.

There are two options for dealing with this problem. First, we can simply use a translation of *hesed*—love, loving-kindness, mercy, steadfast love. Using such a translation repeatedly and consistently will help a congregation identify that term as a technical one with specific meaning. The problem is that no one translation does justice to the depth of the term's meaning and the many different contexts in which it is used in the Bible. Second, the lack of familiarity with *hesed* can be helpful to introduce the new idea to the congregation. But the term cannot just be thrown out in passing and be expected to stick to anyone's ears. If *hesed* is to be used, it will need to be used in ecclesial settings other than just worship and spoken regularly enough in sermons and liturgy that it becomes part of our congregants' vocabulary. It will need to be introduced, not simply spoken, over and over again. But once it becomes part of the church's vocabulary, it will not simply stick to the ears of the laity but become part of the way they name God, self, and the world.

The second issue we need to address if *hesed* is to be useful as an overarching theme in our preaching in countering heterosexism is that the content of the term must not be allowed to seep into theological sentimentality the way, say, *agape* has in some popular and ecclesial settings. In our contemporary culture, the word *love* is understood primarily in emotional, romantic terms; and even when nonromantic love is described, the understanding of that love has been shaped by gushy romantic love. But the scriptural understanding of love, mercy, and kindness that is found in the word *hesed* is a radical, countercultural description of an attitude and form of action toward others. It is not a feeling or an attraction, but a way of being. So here is the rub: over the course of our preaching ministry we must use the term *hesed* in a way that helps people understand other complex doctrines without oversimplifying or domesticating *hesed* itself. We need to shape a habit of using the word in a way that is familiar but never clichéd, or it will lose its power to appropriately name the human condition and God's salvation, and by extension to help battle heterosexism. More infusion of heterosexual concepts into the pulpit of what God's love and Christian love should feel like is the last thing that will help homosexuals know and experience God's *hesed*.

Sermon-Specific Strategies

In individual sermons related to the topics of this chapter, it is important that preachers name heterosexism in relation to anthropological and soteriological issues in ways that invite both gay and straight listeners to experience the fullness of God's blessing, grace, and calling. Assuming most sermons dealing with human nature, sin, and salvation are not focused specifically on heterosexism, the question is how to name gay people, gay issues, and heterosexism in ways that illustrate the sermon's topic as well as counter heteronormativity.

A sermon dealing with human nature and affirming the goodness of *all* beings made in God's image is a perfect opportunity for an illustration that involves a gay person as well as or instead of a straight person. Demonstrating and celebrating God's *hesed* in homosexuals elevates gay hearers' self-esteem and confronts heteronormative hearers' assumptions about God's favor for heterosexuality as the norm of being human.

A sermon dealing with sin offers preachers two different kinds of opportunities in countering heterosexism. The first is to shift talk of homosexuality as sinful to heterosexism as sinful. We must explicitly name heterosexism as a structural sin. Pastors can and should explicitly condemn reparative therapy that tries to fix gay "illness" by helping clients "turn straight." The psychological, spiritual, and at times physical damage done to homosexuals in such approaches is disgusting. Turning the tables so that those approaching homosexuality as a sin are perpetuating sin is a powerful move.

Yet rarely will it be wise to single out heterosexism as the only illustration of sin used in a sermonic move. To do so will likely lead hearers away from the nature of sin to internal thoughts about whether or not homosexuality is a sin, in the sense of a "Thou shalt not . . . ." Instead, if we include heterosexism in the mix of other examples of structural ills that the congregation already assumes to be sinful, heterosexism becomes guilt by association. Describing heterosexism in parallel with oppression of the poor and discrimination based on skin color or gender will do more to persuade hearers with heteronormative world views of its sinfulness than telling them they *ought* to see it differently. Show instead of tell.

A second opportunity for preachers dealing with sin is to name gay people as sinful, just like straight people. A gay person is trapped by selfishness, just like any straight person. Using a gay person to illustrate greed, racial prejudice, pettiness, or hatred is liberating for homosexuals in the sense that it names them as fully human instead of as a human characterized only by their sexuality. Indeed, it shifts their sinfulness from their "unique" sexual orientation (from the perspective of heteronormativity) to their commonality with all people. Again, though, it is important that when exemplifying such "normal" sin with a gay person in sermon, that the homosexual not be isolated. An illustration about a gay man who is ageist can be heard as simply confirming sinfulness rooted in sexual orientation. On the other hand, an illustration about a group of men, some gay and some straight, who mistreat the elderly paints the sin as something unrelated to sexual orientation.

Finally, naming salvation in relation to structural sin allows preachers to counter heterosexism when it is salvation *from* heterosexism instead of homosexuality. Both the oppressed and the oppressor need this salvation. Homosexuals need liberation from the forms of discrimination they have experienced. Heterosexuals need forgiveness and transformation in relation to the privilege, attitudes, and actions they have shared due to the structures of heterosexism. Christ died once *for all*. Preachers must offer God's *hesed* to all.

Sample Sermon: "The End with a Capital E"

IN THE INTRODUCTION, WE suggest that preachers need to review past sermons to look for ways they might have unconsciously promoted heteronormativity or even heterosexism. Part of this review should include looking for places in those sermons where we could have included imagery or discussion to help move the congregation beyond heterosexism. Not only will this step help us better imagine ways we can employ strategies for overcoming heterosexism in future sermons, it invites us to consider revising a sermon that we would preach again to include those elements.

The following sermon on Jeremiah 33:1–16 is such a case. It was composed some years ago as part of a case study for a conversational, cumulative approach to preaching in Allen's book, *The Homiletic of All Believers*.[11] The sermon was intended to be preached on the First Sunday of Advent, Year C (for which Jeremiah 33:14–16 is the Hebrew Bible lesson), for an urban, progressive congregation. The traditional theme of Advent 1 is the *parousia*, or in common parlance, the second coming of Jesus Christ. The Jeremiah text is included in the lectionary because of its eschatological focus and the image of God causing "a righteous Branch to spring up for David" traditionally being interpreted as a prophecy for the coming of Jesus as the messianic son of David.

During the process of doing exegesis as part of the sermon preparation, it became clear that the boundaries of the lection were chosen to fit the traditional theme of Advent 1 and do not do justice to the original content of Jeremiah. As the lection stands, there is no context for understanding why the prophet would say these words. By expanding the passage back to v. 1, we find that Jeremiah is in prison and that this is the "second time" the word of the Lord has come to him. The first time was in a period of great optimism in Judah, and Jeremiah warned of the coming destruction. This second time, in the midst of destruction, Jeremiah is presented as speaking a word of hope, reversal, and restoration, that includes a messiah returning

11. O. Wesley Allen Jr., *The Homiletic of All Believers: A Conversational Approach to Proclamation and Preaching* (Louisville: Westminster John Knox, 2005). The whole case study (89–149) includes four sermons that overlap in terms of preparation and final language and imagery. This particular sermon is found at 116–20.

to the throne of David (not a prediction of the birth of the far-distant Jesus of Nazareth). The full final form of the oracle extends to v. 26. While vv. 14–16 are not enough to do justice to Jeremiah's message, twenty-six verses are likely too much to read in a liturgical context. By extending the passage to vv. 1–16, the congregation gets to hear the broader context with the climax of the lesson still being the language traditionally associated with Advent.

The original sermon on this passage had the basic thrust that while salvation is often thought of in individualistic, pie-in-the-sky terms, it can be understood as a return to normalcy when life has been experienced as some form of turmoil, pain, or oppression. This message, then, fits with the reminder in this chapter that we need to help congregations reconceptualize salvation in structural terms instead of only as forgiveness for breaking commandments on the list of do's and don'ts. While this emphasis in the sermon was not applied primarily to the issue of recognizing heterosexism instead of homosexuality as sinful, it had potential to support this shift with some revisions.

When reviewing this sermon in light of the call to "normalize" homosexuals and same-sex relationships in a heterosexist society, it became clear that the sermon's message could have been used to speak of gay people being treated as "normal" as salvific. While the original sermon does not promote heterosexism, there is certainly nothing in it to counter heteronormativity. Consider the following portion of the original:

> Jeremiah's is a great view of salvation: when God comes there will be an End (with a capital E) to hatred, oppression, sexism, ethnic cleansing, homelessness, war, and so on and so forth, and everything will just be normal. But come on—let's be honest. Aren't all those social evils I've listed (and the hundreds and thousands of others you could add to my lists)—aren't they all normal?

There is nothing wrong with the list of social issues offered here, and indeed, no sermon can deal with all of the social problems with which the church is to be concerned. But simply adding heterosexism to the list here, even with the "so on and so forth," opens the door to more explicit reference to normalizing gay life in other places in the sermon.

Consider another passage in the sermon:

> If you're not sure you would count normalcy as salvation, ask anyone who has entered into remission after battling cancer. Ask any woman who has gotten out of an abusive relationship. Or someone

who has gotten a job after being laid off six months ago. Or an alcoholic who is in recovery. Or someone who starts dating again after the dust of a bad marriage and a worse divorce has settled. Or a neighborhood that rebuilds their home after a tornado has torn it down. Or ask New York City if normal activities don't feel like saving grace in the aftermath of 9/11.

In this passage, we see the tendency to accept heteronormativity at work. The litany of examples of returning to normalcy as salvation works well, rhetorically speaking. But the only two references to relationships—the woman escaping an abusive relationship and the return to dating after divorce—assume heterosexual relationship. The first example does not explicitly refer to a heterosexual relationship, but in the common discourse about abused women, the majority of the congregation would likely assume that I (Wesley) was intending to imply the woman escaped an abusive male (which is what I had in mind when I composed and spoke the words). Adding to this litany an example of homosexual partners being treated as a "normal couple" instead of abnormal would have been a significant message both about normalcy as salvific and the destructive power of heterosexism.

What follows, then, is a thorough revision of this sermon. Any sermon preached nearly a decade later should be thoroughly revised for its new context, but this revision especially has an eye toward including homiletical elements aimed at normalizing homosexuality as part of the very act of proclaiming God's gift of salvation as a return to normalcy. A discussion of what should count as "normal" theologically speaking was part of the original sermon, but it has been revised with an eye to the discussion of the *imago Dei* above as well.

JEREMIAH 33:1–16

¹ The word of the LORD came to Jeremiah a second time, while he was still confined in the court of the guard: ² Thus says the Lord who made the earth, the LORD who formed it to establish it—the LORD is his name: ³ Call to me and I will answer you, and will tell you great and hidden things that you have not known. ⁴ For thus says the Lord, the God of Israel, concerning the houses of this city and the houses of the kings of Judah that were torn down to make a defense against the siege ramps and before the sword: ⁵ The Chaldeans are coming in to fight and to fill them with the dead bodies of those whom I shall strike down in my anger and my wrath, for I have hidden my face from this city because of all their wickedness. ⁶ I am going to bring it recovery and healing; I will heal them and reveal to them abundance of prosperity and security. ⁷ I will restore the fortunes of Judah and the fortunes of Israel, and rebuild them as they were at first. ⁸ I will cleanse them from all the guilt of their sin against me, and I will forgive all the guilt of their sin and rebellion against me. ⁹ And this city shall be to me a name of joy, a praise and a glory before all the nations of the earth who shall hear of all the good that I do for them; they shall fear and tremble because of all the good and all the prosperity I provide for it.

¹⁰ Thus says the Lord: *In this place of which you say, "It is a waste without human beings or animals," in the towns of Judah and the streets of Jerusalem that are desolate, without inhabitants, human or animal, there shall once more be heard ¹¹ the voice of mirth and the voice of gladness, the voice of the bridegroom and the voice of the bride, the voices of those who sing, as they bring thank offerings to the house of the* Lord:

> *"Give thanks to the* Lord *of hosts,*
> *for the Lord is good,*
> *for his steadfast love endures forever!"*

For I will restore the fortunes of the land as at first, says the Lord. *¹² Thus says the* Lord *of hosts: In this place that is waste, without human beings or animals, and in all its towns there shall again be pasture for shepherds resting their flocks. ¹³ In the towns of the hill country, of the Shephelah, and of the Negeb, in the land of Benjamin, the places around Jerusalem, and in the towns of Judah, flocks shall again pass under the hands of the one who counts them, says the* Lord. *¹⁴ The days are surely coming, says the* Lord, *when I will fulfill the promise I made to the house of Israel and the house of Judah. ¹⁵ In those days and at that time I will cause a righteous Branch to spring up for David; and he shall execute justice and righteousness in the land. ¹⁶ In those days Judah will be saved and Jerusalem will live in safety. And this is the name by which it will be called: "The* Lord *is our righteousness."*

THE END WITH A CAPITAL E

No golden ball has dropped in Times Square. We didn't toast one another with champagne last night as we kissed and sang "Auld Lang Syne." There are no college football bowl games today. No ham, collard greens, or black-eyed peas to eat for good luck. But, nevertheless, for the church, today is New Year's Day.

We Christians are an odd lot. We mark time in an odd way. We don't set our spiritual clocks in accordance with the rotation of the earth on its axis or base our church calendar on the phases of the moon or determine our liturgical seasons in relation to the position of the earth in its rotation around the sun. Instead, we structure our time in accordance with ancient time. Church time is determined by Christ's time. We move from expectation to birth to revelation to baptism to transfiguration to ashes to temptation to crucifixion to resurrection to ascension until we receive the Spirit and celebrate the "ordinary" time of the church. And then we do it all over again: Advent to Christmas to Epiphany to Lent to Easter to Pentecost to Ordinary Time and back to Advent again.

We Christians mark time in a strange way. We use this cyclical pattern each and every year, over and over again, to interpret the linear span of time in its entirety, from its beginning when the Spirit swept over the face of the formless void at creation to its End (with a capital E) when the reign of God will be established as world without end. We use this cyclical pattern that begins again today to interpret *our* time as *God's* time, stretching from Alpha to us to Omega.

What's even odder is that each year we mark our beginning by looking ahead to the End (you know, that End with a capital E). God's End. The day of the Lord. The son of the human surfing in on the clouds. Rapture. Judgment and salvation. For all the signs out there right now—sales in the department stores, decorations hanging from the lampposts, carols being played on the radio, and Santa sitting at his post in the mall—for all the signs of Christmas out there, we Christians of all people say, "Hey, wait a minute! One thing at a time. Christmas will come soon enough. But right now is the beginning, so let's start where we're supposed to: at the End. God's End. The time when God will come to us in a new way." That's what the word "advent" means—to come to. We begin our year waiting, expecting, hoping, longing for a vision of God coming to us in a manner that will be so new that time will never be the same again. So new that we can talk about it as the End of what we know and experience now. As new as a babe born in Bethlehem was before we overexposed the stable and saturated the market with shepherds and angel choirs. That's where we begin the new year that the deep blue cloths on the pulpit and table and the four candles in the wreath signify—looking for God's new coming . . . once again.

And, oh, do we ever need it! We need God to come and bring an End (with a capital E) to all the hatred we see around us. An End to unemployment, poverty, and homelessness. An End to suicide bombings. An End to women making less than men in the workplace. An End to dictators who use their subjects for target practice. An end to pollution pouring out of factories, vehicles, and homes into our soil, rivers, and skies. An End to gay couples having to make sure they are in a safe place before they can hold hands. An End to children being shot with bullets zooming out of automatic weapons in schools, malls, and movie theaters. An End to cancer, birth defects, leukemia, strokes, AIDS, heart attacks, diabetes, mental illness, malaria, tuberculosis, and Alzheimer's. We need God to come and say, "Enough is enough." We need God to come to us and say, "The End," and then, "Once upon a time . . . "

People are predicting all over the place when and how God's going to do this. Every generation has its share of apocalyptic forecasters. The Mayan calendar predicted this date. In a dream, God told a televangelist it would be that date. I wish I could just point to others doing this, but we Christians are the worst of all. Every kook who can pronounce the name of Jesus and read the book of Revelation browses news stories on the Internet identifying this and that as signs of the rapture that is to take place on Thursday, at 8:47 p.m. Eastern Daylight Savings time. The *Left Behind* series still sells more copies than toilet paper, which would be a better use for the paper they're printed on: An airplane, headed to London. Suddenly passengers just start disappearing. Ugh!

Maybe there are better visions of God's End, of God's advent, to be found in our tradition, though. For instance, our reading from Jeremiah. Jeremiah offers a vision of God's advent that avoids the extreme of inciting fear. His vision is not a literal prediction of the world stopping existing. It's a vision of the End with a capital E, God's End to the status quo.

Jeremiah was an odd sort. He had been warning Judah that the country was heading toward doom on a one-way camel stampede. This wasn't some ecstatic vision. He simply read the social and political signs and interpreted them theologically. He warned what every reasonable person knew was coming was actually coming: Babylon was going to conquer Judah.

And he interpreted this as a sign of God's judgment. And then it happened. Just as he said. In 587 BCE, Babylon came and laid siege to Jerusalem.

Jerusalem locked down, under attack, being starved out. And what does the king do? He locked up the messenger. Jeremiah said it was going to happen this way, so throw him in prison! But there in his cell, imprisoned by his own king, hated by his own people, with a foreign army beating down the city walls, days away from the temple being razed to the ground and the people being taken into exile, Jeremiah's tone changed. Changed radically. Instead of prophesying, "Thus saith the Lord, 'I told you so,'" Jeremiah began speaking about God's salvation that would come . . . after the destruction. Now mind you, he didn't have grand visions of little Judah somehow miraculously defeating Babylon if it just prayed hard enough. He didn't offer grand visions of God swooping down out of the clouds and rescuing the people at the last minute after the last commercial.

His vision was smaller, simpler—a vision with a small v of the End with a capital E. His vision of God's coming, of God's salvation, was just recovery after the destruction. That's it. Sometime after the attack is over, God will restore the land to normalcy.

Normalcy? That's salvation?

Where there is desolation and despair, there will someday be the normal activities of life again. In place of piles of burnt rubble will be homes and farms. In place of weeping will be people laughing on their way to a wedding or singing on their way to worship. In place of a bottomed-out, stripped-down economy that comes from being the losers in a war, there will be replenished flocks and herds. And in the place of inept, corrupt, oppressive rulers, God will cause a righteous branch to spring up for David. This ruler will act in ways that are just and right.

Jeremiah offers no grand visions of heaven on earth in this prophecy. No dirt roads becoming streets of gold. No cities protected by pearly gates. Instead, there is the simple, compassionate recognition that when life hurts, when life is oppressive, when life is chaotic, when it is a living hell, everyday normal activities can represent an experience of profound and divine grace.

Of course, when compared to the archangel sounding the bugle call to set the four horseman off racing across the planet, the dead being raised and meeting Jesus in the sky, the damned weeping and gnashing their teeth in Hades, and the righteous plucked from their tiny seats on airplanes only to be reseated in the first class section of the messianic banquet, normalcy as salvation sounds just the tiniest bit boring. Really, is everything being normal an adequate description of how we should hope God will save us?

But ask someone who enters remission after battling cancer whether normalcy is salvation, and we'll have our answer. Ask a woman who has gotten out of an abusive relationship and gets to choose her clothes for the day on the basis of what she likes instead what will best hide her bruises, and we'll have our answer. Or ask someone who has gotten a job after being laid off six months ago. Or a child of an alcoholic who is in recovery. Ask a lesbian who lives in a state that finally allows her to marry the woman she loves just like everybody, but where she has also been accused every day and in every way of being abnormal. Ask a New Jersey neighborhood that rebuilds after superstorm Sandy has torn it down whether normalcy seems like a gift from God. Or someone who starts dating again after the dust of a bad marriage and a worse divorce has settled. Or a refugee who returns home to reopen his shop in the marketplace after the cease-fire. Or an orphan who is adopted and becomes part of a family with the same boring routine of homework and chores after school, meatloaf every Tuesday night, and bedtime at 8:30. Ask people who know chaos and fear and violence and sickness and discrimination and isolation if normalcy isn't salvation, and they may just laugh at how naïve we are for even asking such a question.

Still, come on, let's be honest: normalcy's not all it's cracked up to be. After all, cancer and racism and war and miscarriages and depression and gay bashing and addiction and inequity and mountaintop removal mining and shoplifting and bullying and political corruption—these things all seem pretty normal. Just take poverty: wasn't it Jesus who said, "You will always have the poor"? Isn't the whole reason we read Jeremiah as Scripture is that he was addressing a social reality that looked a lot like ours? Sure, the names in the newspaper articles are different, but twenty-six-hundred years later the headlines are pretty much the same: some country invaded a smaller country; somebody stole from someone else; someone has been murdered; a bunch of people are out of work; and so on and so forth. The more things change, the more they stay the same. Isn't all the bad still in the world normal?

Well, we should be careful not to equate routine or habit or repetition over millennia with normalcy ... especially with what is normal in God's eyes. Just because we get used to something doesn't make it normal. People may adapt to living without having enough food or adequate clothing or a decent roof over their heads, but that way of life is not normal. We may be numb to the fact that to stretch our middle-class budgets we buy clothes made in sweatshops in Bangladesh and sold in discount stores that don't provide workers with health insurance, but that doesn't make it normal to use people that way. We may see it as "just the way it is" that some people have to keep their love for someone of the same sex in the closet out of fear of rejection by family, discrimination at work, or violence by some bigot on the street, but that should never be considered a normal way to be in love. A community may get used to the idea that their water supply is filled with chemicals dumped into the river by the factory upstream, but that doesn't make the water normal. We may live in a society where thinness and youth are high values, but there is nothing normal about liposuctions, Botox injections, breast implants, or face-lifts. As residents in the United States we may be comfortable with the fact that we own about 72 percent of the world's automobiles, 61 percent of the world's telephones, and 92 percent of the world's bathtubs, but that doesn't mean that kind of global inequity is normal. A child who has been burned by cigarettes regularly since she was an infant may grow up to marry a violent husband because she has never known anything other than abuse, but she is wrong to think that way of life is normal. Just because we have never known life without all of the awful injuries inflicted on us does *not* mean the way the world is is normal. At least not in the eyes of God, who made us in God's image to love and be loved even as God is love. God desires an End (with a capital E) to all that was not intended to be normal in creation. God's normal is always a new normal.

It's the First Sunday of Advent—New Year's Day for those of us who call ourselves Christian. So maybe we need to make some New Year's resolutions. We have begun by longing for the End (with a capital E). We have begun with a vision of God's salvation, a vision of God coming to bring an End to all the pain and suffering that is anything but a normal in relation to God's hope and will for the world. We need to figure out ways here at the beginning and always how to lean into God's future here and now. How to foreshadow God's standards for a normal world. We need to be resolved to be agents of God's normalcy in a world of brokenness and chaos. When life becomes a living hell, everyday normal activities can represent an experience of divine grace.

A while back there was a small church that struggled with what to do with the fact Christmas fell on a Sunday. Sunday morning was no issue, we

Christians worship on Sunday. But what about Sunday evening? There was youth group and choir rehearsal and Bible Study. It somehow just seemed wrong to cancel church activities on one of the holiest days of the year. But after Christmas Eve and Christmas morning services, they knew attendance would be lower than low.

So somebody suggested that they have sort of a church family gathering in the evening and invite families from the nearby shelter for women and children to join them. People could just bring leftovers to share, and buy some small, inexpensive presents for the children and their mothers. And it wouldn't matter if a lot of church members were there or not.

Well, actually, a lot of people did come. No one brought leftovers, though. They just cooked an extra turkey or ham and brought it instead. It was a big meal. Presents were handed out. Children from the church running around the fellowship hall with children from the shelter while adults sitting around the table talked about this or that.

As the evening wore down and the guests began loading back up on the vans to return to the shelter, one woman came up to a group of the church members. She was obviously about to thank them, but one of the members beat her to it: "Thank you so much for coming to be with us tonight." The woman responded, "Thank you so much for that. Oh, I appreciate the handbag for me and the doll for my daughter. And the meal was delicious. But thank you mostly for helping the two of us feel normal again. It really does seem that Jesus has been born, doesn't it? Thanks for that."

The End, with a capital E. Normal with God's capital N.

2

Ecclesiology

LELA AND SUE HAVE been a couple for ten years. Both were raised in fundamentalist Christian congregations. Because of the negative teachings they heard about homosexuality in those contexts, each has struggled with a whole host of mixed feelings about Christianity and questions as to whether or not there is room for them anywhere in the church. They have come to your church because they have heard that other gay people go there. Their first Sunday, you preach on Gal 3:28, "In Christ there is no slave or free, male nor female . . . for all are one in Christ Jesus." You make clear to the congregation that through baptism all differences between races, sexes, and even sexual orientations are forged into one in both this church and in the universal body of Christ. For the first time since they left fundamentalism, Lela and Sue feel that they may have found a home.

But after attending faithfully for several months, their attendance begins to flag. They volunteer for fewer activities. One day after a service when they are in attendance, you ask Lela if everything is okay. She says that she rarely sees any openly gay people serving as liturgists or assisting at the table, although she is grateful for the times when someone gay does serve. She and Sue hoped they would feel comfortable holding hands inside the sanctuary, but they don't. She says, "We feel welcomed, but not totally at home here, if that makes any sense. . . . The church is open, but maybe not as affirming as we first thought."

How has a church that believes it has done everything in terms of being open *and* affirming not managed to make a gay couple feel at home? As we said in the first chapter, heterosexism is tricky, at times subtle, and always more entrenched than we assume. It exists in ways that well-intentioned preachers and congregations never see but which may be at work in stories like that of Lela and Sue.

In this chapter we will consider the ways that liberal and progressive churches may still unconsciously perpetuate heterosexism in the very structures of church life. To do this we use *hesed* as described in the previous chapter to reimagine the traditional marks of the church (one, holy, catholic, and apostolic) and the traditional practices of the church—*didache, diakonia, koinonia, leiturgia,* and *kerygma* (Greek for teaching, service, fellowship, worship, and proclamation). Since our focus in this work is on preaching, we will only make brief suggestions concerning *diakonia, koinonia,* and *leiturgia,* and then focus more in depth on *kerygma* with *didache*. We combine preaching and teaching because these two functions are not as easily separated for pastors as they were at one time in the life of the church. In today's world, adult Christian education will happen as much if not more in the context of the sermon as anywhere in congregational programming.

If *hesed* marks individuals as made in God's image, then it should certainly be foundational to our corporate life in God—the church. We are not proposing a thoroughgoing ecclesiology, but rather are suggesting ways that some traditional ecclesiological themes might have different real-world consequences when *hesed* becomes the hermeneutical lens for the nonheterosexist church. Before turning to specific marks and practices of the church, however, we need to define some basic words and concepts— the meaning and nature of *ekklesia*, the church as an extension of the *missio Dei*, and the church as the institutional form of our ideas about salvation.

EKKLESIA

Apart from its technical use to name the church, the Greek word *ekklesia* simply designates a group of people who have been summoned—from *kaleō* (to call) + *ek* (out). The church, then, is the collection of those who gather together in the name of Christ, having been summoned or called by God to celebrate, embody, and proclaim the good news of God's grace in Christ through worship, preaching, teaching, service, and fellowship.

Because of human sinfulness and our failure to live by God's *hesed* for one another, being "set apart" has at times been interpreted by Christian groups to mean being "set above" others by God. When living from that sense of superiority, the Christian church has created for itself a history that has been marked by physical, emotional, and spiritual abuse (see below). While it is easy for us to see the results of claiming to be "set above" others in extreme examples, like the homophobia of Fred Phelps's Westboro Baptist Church, it is more difficult to grasp when this mind-set is subtly at work in liberal and progressive congregations. For the liberal church, a sense of superiority, while never intentionally named, may mean being satisfied that it has done all that should be done to live out its welcome to LGBTQI people, especially in comparison to other congregations and denominations. This sense of satisfaction can result in perpetuating heterosexist myopia.

The true nature of being called and gathered in the name of Christ is not to live as better than others, but as a model for a different way of being with one another. Thus, the *ekklesia* is called by God to live in the world according to the values of the reign of God, in the midst of and as a challenge to the status quo (i.e., the world functioning according to the values of the reign of Caesar). In this challenge, however, the church must be mindful that as a human institution it is worldly and thus sinful itself. The church is not the body that judges the holiness of others. As Jesus describes in the parable of the Wheat and Tares (Matt 13:24–30), those called by God "grow" in the same soil and conditions that support life for the rest of the field. Jesus admonishes the disciples to recognize that we finite humans cannot and should not attempt to separate the two; only at the *eschaton*, in God's judgment, will wheat and tares be separated.

Thus the church must live in tension between the imperfect present, in which the values of God's eschatological reign have already begun but have not yet been consummated, and the perfect future when God's vision of life together will be complete. Theologian Dorothee Soelle has written that a church that overemphasizes the already can result in a church that fails at being prophetic, whereas a church too focused on the "not yet" runs the risk of being irrelevant.[1] In the case of the liberal church, which may feel satisfied with its inclusive practices, the balance is tipped to the now/already. However, a reorientation is possible when the church remembers that it is an institutional extension of God's salvific presence in the world. As Jürgen Moltmann argues, "It is not the church that has a mission of salvation to fulfill in the world; it is the mission of the Son and the Spirit through the Father [*sic*] that includes the church, creating the church as it

---

1. Dorothee Soelle, *Thinking about God: An Introduction to Theology* (London: SCM, 1990), 139–40.

goes."[2] Because the church is the extension of the *missio Dei*—the mission of God in and for the world—and not an independent entity, keeping our dependence on God in the forefront of our thinking about what it means to be and act as a church can help keep the progressive church from becoming self-satisfied and content with its progress toward inclusion. The church that understands itself as the extension of the *missio Dei* will be vigilant in looking for the ways it blocks or distorts the steadfast love of God it attempts to live out.

Since the community of the faithful is called by God to live out the *missio Dei*, i.e., God's salvific will in and for the world, we must recall from the opening chapter what the salvific will of God is in relation to homosexuals. There we asserted that salvation means (in part) that we are saved from perpetuating broken relationships and not from our sexual orientations. The focus on establishing and perpetuating right relationships with one another means salvation is a this-worldly rather than otherworldly business. The Christian model for right relationship is seen in the radical "being for others" that defines Christ's life and death. Salvific relationships, then, are those that embody God's *hesed* for all of God's children, relationships that are marked by commitment, mutuality, concern for the well-being of the other, and respect. These qualities pertain as much to our relationships with one another in the body of Christ as they do between partners in intimate relationships.

Having defined *ekklesia,* the *missio Dei,* and the church as the locus of salvation, we turn to re-vision the marks and practices of the church for the nonheterosexist church. We interpret each of the marks as a sign of God's *hesed* and offer suggestions for the ways this mark so interpreted is expressed in *diakonia, koinonia, leiturgia,* and *didache* and *kerygma* in the nonheterosexist church. Consistent with the idea that the church exists not for itself, but as an extension of God's love in Christ for the world, Letty Russell writes: "Although [the marks] are part of a long tradition concerning the identity of the church, the signs are always in need of testing to see if they actually do make clear the mandate of the church to be where Christ is and to share God's work of new creation."[3] Thus, like theological anthropology in the first chapter, the marks of the church can and should be re-visioned in accordance with the new places and new ways we meet

---

2. Jürgen Moltmann, *The Church in the Power of the Spirit* (New York: HarperCollins, 1977), 64.

3. Letty M. Russell, "Why Bother with Church?," in ed. William Placher, *Essentials of Christian Theology* (Louisville: Westminster John Knox, 2003), 243.

Christ. We find that reading the traditional marks of and tasks of the church through the lens of *hesed* offers the liberal and progressive preacher ways to use traditional ecclesiological themes to address lingering heterosexism.

ONE (UNITY IN DIVERSITY)

The mark of the church as "one" is derived from the "oneness" of God, from whom the church receives its mission. God's unity is not the oneness of assimilation, but rather provides for and values the "otherness" of the other as a manifestation of God's loving-kindness.

One way to understand the dialectic of unity in diversity is through the foundational theological metaphor of God as Trinity. Elizabeth Johnson and others have suggested that God's internal relationality (the immanent Trinity) not only preserves difference, but also tells us something about the kinds of values of relating inherent in God. Johnson suggests that the "persons" of the Trinity exist together "as a community of love wherein there is total equality, mutuality and respect for difference."[4] This Trinitarian relationality can be described using the concept *hesed* discussed in Chapter 1: God lives out *hesed* within God's very being.

Then, in turn, God's inner life of *hesed* is the model not only for God's relationship with human beings (the economic Trinity) but also for the unity of the church. In the triunity of God, the Son and the Holy Spirit are not subservient to or assimilated into the Creator, but each exists in its uniqueness *within* the unity of God. Likewise, then, the church's oneness celebrates difference in *hesed*-characterized unity, including differences in sexual orientation.

How does the understanding of God's inner nature as including both unity and "otherness" impact our understanding of what might be going on in the opening scenario? Many liberal congregations strive to be open to homosexuals by taking a stance which diminishes differences between straight and gay people in the faith community. This posture has helped people like Lela and Sue initially find a home in the church, but the same confession is not enough to keep this couple in the church. In many cases a welcoming church still accepts homosexual partners conditionally—the condition being that homosexual couples will not distinguish themselves

4. Elizabeth Johnson, *She Who Is: The Mystery of God in Feminist Discourses* (New York: Crossroads, 1994), 209.

as different. "Difference is allowed if it is minimal and discrete."[5] This unspoken condition is in effect because heterosexual identity (perhaps unconsciously) is still the default assumption of the church when unity is preached.

Lela and Sue are welcomed by the predominantly heterosexual church, but soon find their differences subsumed into the ways they are similar to the heterosexual members of the congregation. This elision is well-intentioned, and falls within a modernist assumption of a shared humanity in which difference disappears in favor of similarity. But this (perhaps unintentional) approach to being community confuses unity with uniformity and conformity and thus translates into a suppression of critical differences.

Such an approach to unity has a long history in society and in the church. In early struggles for racial and sexual equality, the sympathetic white male majority would try to level the playing field by erasing differences between themselves and African Americans or women. While well intentioned, this had those in power defining others on their own terms: they should be considered equal because they are more like us than we have recognized. This stance was open to women and African Americans joining white men in places from which they had once been prohibited, but it was not affirming of who they were in their own identity. Acceptance was based on viewing them through the dominant identity in society, and led to significant tokenizing.

While postmodern interpreters have deconstructed the Enlightenment bias that human nature is defined in terms of what it means to be male, white, and educated, less has been done to deconstruct heterosexist biases in culture's view of human nature. Indeed, heteronormative assumptions about human nature remain alive and well in the church. There simply has not been enough ink spilled or sermons preached deconstructing the heteronormativity of modernist human nature for some churches to have made the move to be not only open but also affirming. We suggest the following practices as a way to make that move.

Diakonia: With respect to honoring difference in its practices of service and outreach to the world, the nonheterosexist church should examine its missions through a variety of probing questions:

---

5. Mary McClintock Fulkerson, *Places of Redemption: Theology for a Worldly Church* (London: Oxford University Press, 2007), 223.

- Which members regularly participate in outreach to the community?

- Do gay members serve "gay causes" more often than heterosexual members?

- Are the manifest differences of some homosexuals uncomfortable to heterosexuals in the church and thus, unintentionally, the gifts of homosexuals are underutilized?

- How does the church identify itself in service? Is it evident to outsiders that this church is welcoming to and affirming of gay people?

Often, men and women who appear homosexual may find that they are unintentionally excluded from the front line of service projects with those who might take offense. For instance, is church leadership reticent to put "out" gay men and lesbians in service work with children and youth, because of the continued (but false) accusations of pedophilia against homosexuals?[6] In terms of service, the nonheterosexist church grounded in God's *hesed*, a love that upholds the difference of the other, will ask itself if/how the oneness of the church has unintentionally promoted uniformity and conformity and thus hinders its attempts to share the liberative message of *hesed* with the world.

Koinonia: A nonheterosexist approach to oneness in the context of fellowship will mean that the church committed to expressing God's *hesed* will find practices of fellowship that invite peoples' differences, even conflicting differences, to be honored through our common bonds. The sermon at the end of the chapter, for instance, describes a scene in which two members of the same congregation, who disagree on the issue of being open and affirming, nevertheless share the Eucharist. Common practices and rituals of the church bring people together in ways that demonstrate their common bonds without asking them to deny their differences.

Leiturgia: At its core, worship is prayer. The oneness of the church calls the body of Christ to pray together with one voice. But celebrating diversity in the midst of our unity means that a wide range of concerns will be lifted up in worship. For the church celebrating diversity in terms of sexual orientation, then, issues that are especially important to gay members of the church should be included in the prayers of the whole people. Moreover, these concerns should be a part of the whole liturgical drama of

6. See Chapter 3 for a fuller discussion of this issue.

worship, not simply mentioned tangentially in a prayer here or there or in a sermon every once in a while.

Also, the mark of oneness in a nonheterosexist church means gay members of the congregation should be full participants in leading worship. They must serve as liturgists, ushers, and servers on a regular basis and must not just be brought forward in a tokenizing fashion to lead a piece of liturgy when "gay issues" are on the table.

Kerygma and Didache: Our definition of the "oneness" of the church as unity without assimilation is based on difference as essential to the very nature of the triune God. This means that pastors will need to help the congregation better understand trinitarian theology in order to better envision the church as one.

While the theological sentiment of ecclesial unity is easy to name, it is difficult to teach and proclaim the nature of the church in such a way that the church lives into its reality of being this *one* church. While we can agree with Paul that the body of Christ, like the human body, is made up of many members (1 Cor 12:12–31; Rom 12:4–8), we focus more easily on the one body and less on the differences in functions necessary to make it work.

Loving the other as "other" means being willing to open oneself to discomfort by listening to ideas and accepting behavior that are not one's own. As noted in the previous chapter, this respect for difference does not translate into an uncritical "anything goes" mentality in terms of ethics. *Hesed* is the standard by which we judge behavior—ours and others'—and it is the basis on which we open ourselves to the discomfort that comes with differences that we find challenging. To preach or teach the oneness of the church in a way that moves beyond heterosexism, our sermons must explicitly name in illustrations same-sex couples holding hands in the sanctuary, the blessings and difficulties of being same-sex parents, and the realities of being gay in an increasingly tolerant but not yet affirming world. In other words, we must make concrete for the heterosexual majority, the homosexual "other" as *one of "us."* The preacher must offer a vision of the oneness of the church that is not separate and equal but different and together.

HOLY (WHOLENESS)

Historically, holiness was a category of being distinguished from the clean (which is a state of normalcy) and the unclean (which is contagious). To be holy (i.e., to be of a special level of purity) is to be set apart. In biblical times, only God was considered holy by nature, and in turn God ordained that other things and people would be set apart as holy. Over time in the church, the category of holiness shifted from ritual to moral purity. The mark of the church as holy, then, has been understood to indicate that God has set the church apart to be pure as God is pure.

The problem with this understanding of holiness is that the purity of God has too often been limited to the nature of God as Spirit. This way of interpreting God's holiness that is passed on to God's holy church has served as the rationale for the church's long-standing denigration of the material world, a bias affecting human bodies together with all of nature.[7] With those in power (i.e., heterosexual males) viewing themselves as those most inclined toward spirit, the bias against those seen as differently embodied has contributed to gender discrimination, racism, ageism, ableism, and, of course, heterosexism.

Letty Russell offers a corrective to this view by arguing that the mark of the church as *holy* should best be understood as the call to the church to help all God's creatures live *wholly*. Dwight Hopkins similarly argues that interpreting God's holy nature as complete—whole—means the end of the mind-body dualism that has characterized ecclesial history. He writes, "One cannot love the body of Christ and hate human flesh."[8]

The church's dualistic bias favoring mind/spirit over bodies diminishes the nature of God as immanent, the greatest example of which is God's incarnation as Jesus of Nazareth. As the man Jesus, God experiences the full spectrum of bodily life, from birth to suffering and death. In addition the Gospels tell us that God cares a great deal about the physical condition of human bodies, as Jesus feeds, heals, and comforts vulnerable people. God incarnate, the radically immanent divine, creates the conditions of thriving for God's creatures. Thus we can say that God's *hesed* as revealed in the person and works of Jesus Christ embraces the whole person as the integration of body, mind, and spirit. This wholeness, this holiness, includes our sexual nature.

The nonheterosexist church, participating in the *missio Dei,* seeks to create the conditions of thriving—of physical and relational wholeness—that are a reflection of the holiness of the immanent God who values the

---

7. Russell, "Why Bother with Church?," 245. See also our discussion in Chapter 1.

8. Dwight N. Hopkins, *Being Human: Race, Culture, and Religion* (Minneapolis: Fortress, 2005).

thriving of the whole creature. One challenge for the progressive church that pursues the wholeness of its members is to extend its welcome to homosexual persons beyond being open to the *idea* of homosexuality, in order to affirm appropriate public physical *expressions* of it. Too often the church says it accepts gay persons but really expects them not to act *too* gay, not to be wholly who they are. Just as appropriate physical expressions of heterosexuality in the church (and in the culture at large) pass by unnoticed by most people, so the nonheterosexist, holy church seeks to normalize expressions of affection and relationship between homosexual partners. Such an affirming stance continues to dismantle the mind/body dualism of the church that has kept sexism and racism alive but unspoken. For Lela and Sue, being welcomed in wholeness needs to include freedom to express their love for one another in the sanctuary: holding hands, an arm around a shoulder in the pew, a kiss "hello" or "goodbye." God's immanent nature and affirmation of the wholeness of human beings challenges the church to continue to seek out and reform the ways it tacitly lifts up reason, thought, and the spiritual over against desire, physicality, materiality, and bodies. While the church may have effectively countered this dualism in challenging its sexism and racism, the situation described in the opening scenario reminds us that homosexual signs of affection, as expressions of God's *hesed*, remain taboo in the church.

Diakonia: In service, honoring the wholeness of homosexual persons in the nonheterosexist church means countering strong prejudices against homosexuality in the world outside the church. The current ban on gay Boy Scout leaders is a case in point. Boy Scout troops are largely (70 percent) sponsored by religious institutions, including liberal and progressive churches. The homophobic assumption that homosexual sexual orientation is both contagious and includes pedophilia keeps gay men from serving youth as Scout leaders. While gay Scouts are now allowed into the organization, they will not find in it role models for living as an out gay man. Instead, gay youth will see that homosexuality should at best be invisible and at worst shunned.

Thus, when considering service-oriented activities and commitments of the church, we must ask: Does the church support local, national, and international missions that are directly or indirectly homophobic? Has the church thoroughly investigated the beliefs and practices of the groups it aids in the same ways it did when it took aim at South African apartheid?

Koinonia: In fellowship, sharing the loving-kindness of God will include sacrifice for the other. As we noted in Chapter 1, when the dominant group demands sacrifice of those not in power it is oppression. Sacrifice in the sense of giving up privilege on behalf of the oppressed, however, is a valuable element of communal life. To live up to the mark of holiness as promoting wholeness, then, some church members may need to sacrifice their comfort established by heteronormativity. They cannot simply be open to gay brothers and sisters in the faith as sexual beings in theory only. To welcome the gay persons as "others" means affirming their wholeness as embodied, relational beings who deserve the same freedoms of expression as their heterosexual brothers and sisters in the body of Christ. Otherwise, they are not truly part of the fellowship but token representatives on the margins of the community.

Leiturgia: For many congregations, the concept and language of holiness appears in liturgy at least twice each week: first in the Lord's Prayer, where we lift up God's name as hallowed, and second in the creed, where we affirm that the church is holy. For the laity, though, the connection between these two claims is tentative and implicit at best. In the liturgy, we need to find ways to make the connection between God's and our holiness more explicit.

Such explicit connectional work will then allow us to give thanks for ways the church's holiness is an instrument of God's making whole. Wholeness in worship implies loving God with all our heart, soul, strength, and mind. This means not simply being intellectually or emotionally whole in worship but also physically whole. Worship is an embodied act of offering God adoration. If gay members are implicitly expected to act, sound, look, and/or dress straight in worship, they are hindered from offering their "whole and made whole" selves to God. The church must find ways to invite all people in worship, including LGBT members of the congregation, to be (or better to become) whole in participating in the "work of the people."

Kerygma and Didache: Preaching and teaching about the church as holy has a different problem associated with it than the task of preaching the church's oneness. The problem with oneness was correcting a misunderstanding in which unity implied sameness. Even though we have offered a re-vision of the traditional understanding of the holiness of the church above, the problem with preaching and teaching this shift is that most people in the pews have little concept of holiness in the first place. Holiness is not a category mainline Christians think about much beyond considering

Mother Teresa to be holy (as an example of moral purity that goes beyond anything we are) or thinking about someone who is hyperpious as being "holier than thou." They probably do not recognize when they pray each week, "hallowed be thy name," that they are lifting up God's holiness, and they certainly do not spend much time reflecting on what it means to affirm that the church is a holy institution. This means there is not a view of the church as holy that must be corrected so much as it must be initiated. The question, then, is how in our teaching and preaching do we introduce the doctrine that the church is holy in the sense of participating in God's work of making and celebrating our wholeness?

One approach is to preach and teach about the holiness of the church in relation to the immanent and incarnate God who values human embodiment. Preaching the immanent and incarnate God can mean prophetically unmasking the surprising ways that dualism continues to function in the liberal and progressive church. We remember that our sexuality is an inseparable element of our created nature, as we discussed in Chapter 1, which means that valuing embodiment will mean valuing physical expressions of everyone's whole selves. To break down taboos related to homosexual affectional practices will mean being willing to proclaim that human sexuality in general, heterosexuality and homosexuality, is a part of our whole, created good. The contemporary church has not done a good job of offering a Christian ethic of sexuality. One rooted in *hesed* will allow the church to offer wholeness beyond the heteronormative approach to sexuality in the church's past.

Similar to preaching the other marks of the church through the lens of *hesed*, preaching the church as holy also means reminding the congregation that God's loving-kindness is sacrificial, and then describing what sacrifice for the well-being of the other—*truly* other—might mean in the context of overcoming heterosexist dualism in the church. It will be important to demonstrate for the congregation how such sacrificial language in the church has usually been misused to require those oppressed to suffer on behalf of the powers that be. This will allow us to then offer them a view of the biblical tradition of sacrifice as the reverse of this—those in power sacrifice for the good of the marginalized. In this case the heterosexual majority must be invited to give up its centrist position so that those of whom society makes less can become whole in God's grace. Indeed, both gay and straight people become more whole when balance is restored in the community through such sacrifice. It is in this way that the church can be presented as set apart from the world.

CATHOLIC (MUTUALITY)

On first appearance, "catholic" seems to be synonymous with the mark of the church as "one." The traditional affirmation that the church is catholic (universal), however, moves beyond the mark of oneness (unity) in the sense that its scope is global. The church as catholic is to be the same everywhere and always. As Ephesians puts it, "There is one body and one Spirit, just as you were called to the one hope of your calling, one Lord, one faith, one baptism, one God and Father [*sic*] of all, who is above all and through all and in all" (4:4–6).

While this biblical ideal sounds worthy as a goal of the church's continued mission, there are several aspects of the traditional understanding of catholicity that bear re-visioning as we examine the mark of the church for heterosexist implications. In truth, the mark of catholicity has a bloody history. The church often strived to establish the global universality of the faith through the tools of coercion and violence, as it accompanied seventeenth- and eighteenth-century European, and nineteenth-century American, colonial conquests into "dark" continents. From these missions, what came to be considered the universal nature of the church was in fact a very particular cultural expression of what the church was and should be—i.e., the catholic church bore the face of the Anglo-European colonizer. This exclusivist Christianity based its violent spread on the belief that no measure was too extreme to "save" the souls of indigenous people.

In place of this sort of uniformity, we propose that the church's catholicity be understood as mutuality. This shift names that what is universal in and about the church is the presence of God's *hesed* always, everywhere, and already; and it names the call for the church to embrace and manifest mutual relationship characteristic of *hesed* in its mission in and throughout the world.

In other words, mutuality requires that we come to know and spread God's love across the globe through *discovery* rather than domination of the "other." Among the many attributes characteristic of *hesed* is a vulnerability to the "other." Catholicity as mutuality means being vulnerable to the global "other" to the extent that we are willing to put aside our own agendas when those agendas hinder relationships of *hesed*. Attempts to force on others a message of a divine love denies the wholeness and integrity of other children of God and is a perversion of the gospel of God's love itself.

The power dynamics of imperial, colonial Christianity are as evident in the history of heterosexism in the church as they are in the missionary movements of the past. As mission work intended to spread Western Christianity universally was a tool of colonization of the Anglo-European world view, culture, behavior, and interests, heterosexism in the church has meant "offering" salvation to homosexuals by forcing them to look and act like heterosexuals. This heterosexist approach to universalizing the church has included using tools of coercion and even violence in "saving" individuals from the "darkness" of homosexuality (for example, reparative therapy). However, there are subtler, even unconscious, forms of maintaining heteronormative universality that may appear even in progressive churches:

- preaching that fails to prophetically denounce spiritual, mental, and physical violence against homosexuals in the church and in the community;

- unexposed heterosexist assumptions in our theological anthropologies that tacitly reinforces the deficiency, perceived sinfulness, or perverse nature of LGBT persons over against heterosexuals;

- unintentionally tokenizing LGBT people by using them as sermon examples for the exceptional welcoming nature of the individual church or having them serve irregularly at the table for the same reasons;

- rejecting LGBT people implicitly by adopting a Don't Ask, Don't Tell posture with respect to ordination.

In all of these instances, implicit or explicit hierarchies of value that assume what should be normative or universal remain intact.

In a re-visioning of the mark of catholicity in terms of mutuality, we suggest engaging two major theological themes. First, we turn again to the nature of the Trinity. Mutuality, rather than domination and subordination, defines the relationship among the persons of the immanent Trinity. This metaphor for God's nature serves as a model for the church's nature. As God values both difference and equality in Godself, so should the church value diversity and equality in the church. The words of an often-quoted African proverb sheds light on the kind of identity of the church as catholic we advance here: "I am because we are." The health of the universal church is predicated on the well-being of all who comprise it. This well-being can only occur when there is an ideological shift from a dominant "I" to a collective "we" in the construction of identity. In the case we are making here, the dominant "I" has most often worn the face of the heterosexual majority, unintentionally assimilating the homosexual minority into itself in ways we name above. This understanding of catholicity as mutuality is a global interpretation of the unity in diversity we discussed above under the mark of the church as one.

A second theological theme that helps reinterpret the mark of catholicity as mutuality is the omnipresence of God. If we believe the presence of Christ and love of God is already everywhere, then the catholicity of the church is sought through an ongoing process of *discovering* how God is revealed in all places and times rather than one which superimposes assumptions about how God *should* be present from one context onto another. This is to say that the character of catholicity in the nonheterosexist church actively resists the idea that any form of conquest or domination of the "other" is the appropriate processes by which the universal nature of the church is manifested. Rather, the universality of the church is the product of encounters between equals, whether those equals are individuals or cultures. Relationships of mutuality between diverse equals are relationships in which all members are open to being changed in the process of discovery. Thus creating relationships of mutuality that characterize *hesed* will require a celebration of difference in the community and a sacrifice of privilege for the sake of the marginalized. Such mutuality as the mark of catholicity suggests a posture of shared authority in the various ministries of the church.

Diakonia: The community of Christ grounded in the value of mutuality recognizes that there is much to learn from being in service to others. Service will mean not only going where the Spirit leads but learning to see and hear the work of the Spirit everywhere already. While the nonheterosexist church may be adept at seeing and addressing heterosexism locally, in its congregation, and in its and community, the work of the church is global. It must hear the stories from outside itself and be changed by them into action. For instance, is the church that advocates for citizenship for the undocumented worker also advocating for the right to citizenship for the gay partners of those workers? Does the church hear and respond to the voices of gay Ugandans as they endure increasing numbers of violent homophobic acts against them in their own country?

Koinonia: "Tolerance" of difference does not meet the measure of mutuality in community. In the local congregation, larger denominational structures, and ecumenical and global connections, straight Christians must seek out and be in meaningful, reciprocal relationship—relationship characterized by *hesed*—with LGBT Christians, or we have divided the body of Christ. How many congregations that claim to be "open and affirming" have worship in which the nave seems to be segregated with gay members sitting here and straight members sitting there? Passing the peace in the church should lead to deeper conversation with "others," and not be the totality of contact with them.

Leiturgia: The universality of the church is foundational to worship—Christian communities across the globe read the same Scripture, recite the same creeds, say some of the same prayers, and practice the same sacraments. To focus on a sacrament as an example, never are we more in fellowship with others in the body of Christ than when we share the Eucharist and express symbolically our communion with God and one another. For the couple in the opening scenario, however, seeing LGBT members of the congregation serving at the table was not a common situation but rather a special occasion. When homosexuals stand at the table, is it part of a normal rotation or is the church demonstrating something about itself, its openness? Are LGBT people integrated into the fabric of worship and community or are there still ways in which they might be tokenized? The sermon below lifts up the table as a place in the church where differences are not shed so much as they coexist in mutual relationship.

Kerygma and Didache: Rather than understanding themselves as the sole interpreters of the gospel, preachers and teachers in the nonheterosexist church understand that they offer one voice amid a community of voices making meaning of the gospel. If catholicity is best defined as mutuality in the larger context of *hesed*, then preaching will be an additive process wherein preachers know that their task is to add their voices to an ongoing historical and contemporary conversation about the presence of Christ in the world. This is not to say that preachers do not have a special authority rooted in their study on behalf of the community, but it is to say that their authority does not trump the work of the Spirit through the lives and voices of those they serve.[9]

---

9. For a conversational approach to preaching in this vein, see O. Wesley Allen Jr., *The Homiletic of All Believers* (Louisville: Westminster John Knox, 2005).

Even if I am the primary preacher Sunday after Sunday in my congregation, I must find ways to authentically bring the voices of others into
my sermons. I cannot do this without being in mutual relationship with
"others" from whom I am willing to learn and with whom I am called to
change. For instance, to what degree can I identify the ways my *preaching*
is informed and changed by the realities of people like Lela and Sue? If I
am a straight pastor, can I be in true mutual relationship with homosexual
members of the church without being prepared to sacrifice my comfort
with the status quo to preach on the kinds of differences that distinguish
homosexual relationships from heterosexual relationships and not simply emphasize the similarities so that "they" look like "us"? Can I be in
true mutual relationship with straight members of my church if I do not
challenge the church to examine its heterosexist biases? Am I prepared to
speak out against my own denomination when the denomination qualifies
God's call to church leadership and ordained ministry on the basis of sexual
orientation?

APOSTOLICITY
(CONSISTENCY WITHOUT STAGNATION)

As a mark of the church, apostolicity has traditionally been used to claim
that the church in any period is a continuation of the apostolic church and
its faith, i.e., the first-generation church founded and led by the apostles.
It is an institutional expression of the communion of saints. There are two
things at stake in this claim: in any historical era 1) the church's message
and mission are consistent with that of the early church; and 2) the church's
authority is rooted in this consistency. The two most obvious expressions of
these assertions are the use of the canon as the primary source of theological authority and ordination rooted in apostolic succession—i.e., clergy are
literally or symbolically in direct succession with the apostles (especially
Peter) through the laying on of hands by each generation (particularly bish-
ops) ordaining the next.

As a mark of the church, then, apostolicity guarantees that the church
of each generation is not creating itself *ex nihilo* in any way it sees fit
but is grounded in the teaching of the apostles (as expressed in the New
Testament canon) who were called and sent out (Greek: *apo* + *stello*, the
literal meaning of apostle) by Christ, in the tradition passed down from
the apostles through the generations of the church. The church is always

and everywhere an extension of the teaching of those who knew Christ firsthand.

The problem with apostolicity is that it has often been interpreted and applied as a vice clamped onto the church by those in power who resist a change to the status quo that would threaten their station. For example, as seen in Scripture, Jesus chose men as apostles; thus apostolicity has been interpreted to mean that only men can be ordained.

But alongside apostolicity, Protestants declare *Ecclesia reformata, semper reformanda*—the church reformed, always to be reformed. Paul Tillich calls this approach to the church's being the Protestant Principle, i.e., "the divine and human protest against any absolute claim made for a relative reality."[10] Thus, self-criticism is woven into the very fabric and faith of the church. "The church always to be reformed" is protection against idolatry of any source of the church's faith or expression of the church's identity and works, including the apostolic church. This principle is active in the fact that much of the church has moved (albeit far too slowly) to embrace women as ordained ministers. The argument is made that the exclusion of women from apostolic ministry was an oppressive feature of the early church that never truly fit with the *content* of the apostolic faith and mission. Patriarchal cultures and the idolatry of the masculine have prevented the church from fully living out the gospel of Jesus Christ. By ridding the church of this sin, our practice better lives up to the apostolic faith. The change, then, is anything but a whim of the modern era, and apostolicity as a mark of the church can be considered a key part of the basis for the move in that reform is brought about by returning to and reinterpreting the canon as the primary source of the faith transmitted to us by the apostolic church. As reform happens, then, it does so by arguing that the church can be consistent even as it reveals suppressed elements of the apostolic faith.

Apostolicity as a mark of the church properly re-visioned, therefore, is a paradox of consistently holding onto the authoritative ideal of the past in order to reform constantly the practices of the past. Such tension is a key element of overcoming heterosexism in the church.

One of the primary strategies for promoting and maintaining heterosexism in the church is the use of Scripture. It is argued that the canon, as passed down to us from the apostolic church, has several explicit condemnations of homosexual behavior (Lev 18:22; 20:13; Rom 1:27; 1 Cor 6:9; 1 Tim 1:10) as well as stories presenting homosexual behavior as sinful

---

10. Paul Tillich, *The Protestant Era* (Chicago: University of Chicago Press, 1948), 163.

(Gen 19:1–11; Judges 19:16–24). In contrast, there are no passages explicitly commending homosexual behavior or relationships in Scripture. Thus, it is argued, to be consistent with the apostolic tradition we must reckon homosexuality to be a sin, condemn homosexuals, and exclude them from various practices, functions, and offices of the church. This version of apostolicity, however, is idolatrous. Neither bibliolatry nor biblicism are synonyms for apostolicity.

In contrast, a primary strategy for breaking the oppressive bonds of heterosexism in the church has been to claim a different understanding of apostolicity as the basis of reform. This strategy has taken several forms of returning to the canon as authoritative while opposing the interpretation offered above. First, there has been much effort put into critical readings of the texts listed above to show that some of them are not really about homosexuality (for instance, the story of Sodom and Gomorrah is really dealing with the ancient understanding of hospitality and honor, not gay sex) or are about same-sex sexual behavior that is different from the mutual, consensual, loving relationships of contemporary homosexuals (for instance, some of the Pauline references more likely focus on pederasty than partners of the same age). This strategy is persuasive in relation to some of the passages named above, but less so in relation to others.[11]

Second, there have been attempts to claim that some biblical stories used veiled imagery and language to present homosexual relationships in a positive light (for example, David and Jonathan or Ruth and Naomi).[12] Rarely is this strategy exegetically persuasive. Nevertheless, along with the first strategy, it shows an appropriate attempt to work within the apostolic tradition while reforming the interpretation and application of that tradition.

11. Alice Ogden Bellis and Terry Hufford, *Science, Scripture and Homosexuality,* (Cleveland: Pilgrim, 2002), 93–122; Dan O. Via and Robert Gagnon, *Homosexuality and the Bible: Two Views* (Minneapolis: Augsburg Fortress, 2003), 4–18; Horace L. Griffin, *Their Own Received Them Not: African American Gays and Lesbians in Black Churches,* (Eugene, OR: Wipf and Stock, 2006), 64–69; Pamela Beattie Jung and Ralph F. Smith, *Heterosexism: An Ethical Challenge* (Albany, NY: State University of New York Press, 1993), 80.

12. Thomas M. Horner, *Jonathan Loved David: Homosexuality in Biblical Times* (Philadelphia: Westminster, 1978); John Boswell, *Same-Sex Unions in Premodern Europe* (New York: Vintage, 1994), 135–37; David M. Halperin, *One Hundred Years of Homosexuality* (New York: Routledge, 1990), 83; Rebecca Alpert, "Finding Our Past: A Lesbian Interpretation of Ruth," in eds. Judith A. Kates and Gail Twersky Reimer, *Reading Ruth: Contemporary Women Reclaim a Sacred Story* (New York: Ballantine, 1994), 91–96.

A third strategy employed by many progressive theologians and theological ethicists holds that the final authority for all interpretation is the criterion of unconditional love at the core of the gospel.[13] This is the best of the three approaches, and one that can ground the practice of moving beyond heterosexism in our preaching. The argument for the finality of the love ethic names that the apostolic tradition (including the canon) has sinful, oppressive elements in it (such as patriarchy and heterosexism) that are expressions of human finitude and cultural conditioning. These elements, however, must always be weighed over against the core, overarching, and transcendent message of God's good news for the world. Ronald J. Allen describes this theological criterion in relation to preaching as "appropriateness to the gospel." He writes,

> The church seeks to determine the degree to which every biblical text, Christian doctrine and practice, ethical action, personal and social situation, and every voice in the preaching conversation is appropriate to (or consistent with) the gospel. Is this text, etc., appropriate to the news of God's unconditional love promised to each and all and God's call for justice for each and all as the church comes to know these realities through Jesus Christ?[14]

In this book, we have been using the term *hesed* to name the core message of the gospel. Any biblical or theological expression of the nature of humanity, the mission of the church, or God's will and desire for the world must be weighed as to whether it accords with God's *hesed* and our potential for and calling to extend *hesed* to one another. In terms of countering heterosexism, then, the church does best when it 1) recognizes and explicitly declares that those texts and traditions which condemn homosexual behavior are counter to God's loving-kindness and our love of neighbor, and 2) views the potential for mutual respect and concern for the other within homosexual relationships as more consistent with the apostolic faith's core understanding of God's character and the Christian ethic of love.

Diakonia: Are there places or ways that the church should serve that are in keeping with its commitment to its care for the other but into which it has failed to enter because it is stuck in old, heteronormative patterns? For instance, when we consider our outreach ministries, who stays at our

---

13. For example, Dan O. Via and Robert Gagnon, *Homosexuality and the Bible,* 29–39.

14. Ronald J. Allen, *Interpreting the Gospel: An Introduction to Preaching* (St. Louis: Chalice, 1998), 83.

emergency shelters and eats in our soup kitchens? Are these welcoming places for out gay/lesbian individials and couples or transgendered persons to stay or to eat, or do these missions still support heteronormativity? While progressive churches may have made great strides in things like sponsoring the LGBT community choir or providing a booth at the local gay pride festival, there may still be implicit heterosexist biases at work in other areas of ministry that reflects a continued fear of the other.

Koinonia: Part of the way the church has lived out apostolicity is to set the boundaries of the community of faith in a way that reflect the boundaries of the early church. At its best this has involved the requirement of baptism as a sign and promise of forgiveness of sins and the gift of the Holy Spirit for membership in the church. At its worst, it has been used to exclude people from membership and some members from leadership based on reasons forced upon (instead of found in) the apostolic content of the good news of Jesus Christ.

This sort of exclusion has too often been the practice in relation to homosexuals. Use of a few proof texts seemingly condemning homosexuality have been used to ban gay men and lesbians from the fellowship of the church. But when we take the story of the inclusion of the Gentiles in the early church found in Acts 10—11, 15 as the model for our consistency in setting boundaries instead of the standard heterosexist proof texts, we act differently. Peter does not initiate the process by which Cornelius and his household is converted and baptized. He follows God's initiative and notes that if God has given the Spirit to the Gentiles, who is he to say they cannot be baptized and thus become brothers and sisters in the messianic community? The church follows Peter's logic later in deciding that Gentiles need not be circumcised (i.e., become Jews) in order to be Christian.[15] The church today likewise should admit people based not on their sexual orientation but on whether they manifest the Spirit's leading them to be baptized and be a part of the fellowship of the redeemed. Put differently, if God is active in a gay person's life, who are straight people to tell them they must "choose" heterosexuality to be Christian?

Leiturgia: Often the unfortunate translation of consistency in liturgy is stagnation in the form of the statement, "This is the way we have always done it." "Tradition" becomes a matter of comfort of the assembled rather

---

15. See Luke Timothy Johnson, *Scripture and Discernment: Decision Making in the Church* (Nashville: Abingdon, 1996) for a thorough description of the Acts texts as a basis for following the guidance of the Spirit in contemporary church life.

than a reflection of the beliefs of the church and the challenge of the gospel. "The way we have always done it" may mean keeping gay people in roles that the heterosexual majority is comfortable with but which limit the visibility of homosexuals—seen but not heard. For example, there is a church in which the flowers on most Sundays were arranged by two gay men in the congregation. These two men, however, were never seen serving Communion at the table on which those flowers sat or leading worship in other ways. The two men may have not wished to be more visible in the worship service, but it is important to ask: Were there social conditions in the church that made them more comfortable working behind the scenes instead of in front of the congregation? Do out gays and lesbians serve as greeters at the beginning of worship—are they the first faces and voices visitors experience when they come to our church for the first time? Seeking consistency that reflects the unconditional love and ethic of justice of the gospel means disrupting cherished social patterns that inertia and fear have left unchallenged. This kind of disruption ensures that our practices reflect our beliefs.

Kerygma and Didache: We argue above that one of the primary strategies for promoting and maintaining heterosexism in the church is the use of Scripture, and we advocate reading all biblical texts through the lens of the love ethic. Similarly, preachers and teachers should keep an eye out for texts that do not explicitly address heterosexism but do present the love ethic in a way that can inform our thinking about overcoming heterosexism. For example, the sermon that ends this chapter uses as its contemporary image a church at odds over and debating the inclusion of gays and lesbians in the community. The love ethic informing the sermon comes in the form of Paul's letter to the Philippians: "Be of the same mind. . . ." In the midst of debating these issues, we should be emptying ourselves, humbling ourselves, for those with whom we are fervently arguing. "Be of the same mind." "Let the same mind be in you that was in Christ FJesus."

HOMILETICAL STRATEGIES

In our discussion of *kerygma* in relation to each of the four marks of the church, we have already moved into the realm of homiletical strategies and need not repeat those suggestions here. A few added comments, however, will be helpful to synthesize a nonheterosexist homiletical approach related to ecclesiology and will set up our sample sermon.

Longitudinal Strategies

We preachers may have few times we are called on to preach specifically about the four essential marks of the church or the five core practices of the church, but every Sunday's sermon is potentially an ecclesiological sermon. This is true simply by the fact that the sermon is offered in the church by the church to the church. In this sense, then, the proclamation of any aspect of God's good news contributes to the formation of community

Added to this contextual issue is a scriptural one. The different marks and practices of the church are implied almost weekly in the scriptural texts on which we preach. Every time a community is represented in a text—be it Israel, the disciples, or the Corinthian house churches—there is a potential homiletical connection and analogy to be drawn to the character and life of the church today. Even when the theological emphasis of passages involving such communities is elsewhere, the passage has implications for congregational identity. Never is this more obvious than in epistle readings of the lectionary where Paul is explicitly trying to shape the communal existence of the early church.

The ecclesial context of sermons and the connections with communities in and behind Scripture passages on which our sermons are based mean almost all of our sermons are at least tentatively related to ecclesiology, and the preacher should be aware of this potential, because it means that every sermon can contribute to constructing the community of faith as a heterosexist or a nonheterosexist institution and fellowship of believers.

When it comes to offering a nonheterosexist ecclesiological vision in our preaching, we should refrain from exhorting the congregation about what it ought to do. Exhortation begins with the assumption that we have failed at something. This of course may be an accurate assessment of the current state of the church in relation to heterosexism. As there is a radical difference between diagnosis and cure, however, there is also a difference between analyzing our audience and our communication with it. Telling a congregation what kind of church we *should* be will evoke more guilt or resistance than inspiration and transformation.

It is better to name the church as characterized by unity in diversity, empowering wholeness, mutuality, and consistency without stagnating *ontologically*. After all, in the Nicene Creed we say we believe in the one, holy, catholic, and apostolic church; we do not say that we believe the church *ought* to be the one, holy, catholic, and apostolic community. These marks (and practices) name what the church already *is* as created and defined by God.

There is of course tension between the institutional church, with its mixture of saintliness and sinfulness, and the theological ideal of the church, so that the marks and practices as described above are both descriptive and prescriptive. But this is the eschatological reality of the already/not yet that defines all of Christian experience. By proclaiming the church as ontologically defined by these marks and practices, we inspire the congregation to live into its already-given but yet-to-be-completed identity. Instead of telling us who we could be, sermons tell us who we *really* are. Tell us enough times and we'll start to believe it; tell us a few more times and we will be it. Interpret these ontological characteristics of the church enough times, from enough perspectives in relation to heterosexism, and the church will become the nonheterosexist church it is.

One caveat should be offered to preachers, however, in relation to this strategy of naming the church ontologically. We should not make church seem too easy. The church will always gather as a communion of both saints and sinners—indeed as a communion of individuals, all of whom are both saintly and sinful. We will always be a community of already and of not yet. Above when we say "tell us enough times and we'll start to believe it," we should be clear there will never be enough times so that we can finally say, "Enough." The history of the church is a story of faithful progress through the centuries—that is, faithful progress in terms of unity in diversity, promoting wholeness, mutuality, and consistency without stagnation mixed with backwards steps of unfaithful conflict, oppression, colonization, and idolatry. As a human institution, the church still struggles with sexism, racism, and classism. We should expect the struggle with heterosexism to be a long one as well.

Sermon-Specific Strategies

In addition to the ways we have discussed kerygma above in relation to interpreting the marks of the church in service of dismantling heterosexism, one simple homiletical strategy for the individual sermon stands above all others in accomplishing this work: we must make sure to include in our individual sermons homosexual individuals, couples, and families as integral members of the community in sermonic imagery presenting the church at its best to itself. When we preach on ecclesiological topics, we should be intentional about presenting gay and straight members together in images of leading and following in the church that illustrate oneness, holiness, catholicity, and apostolicity. When we name the work of the church, we should find images in which we present gay and straight members together in the work of *diakonia, koinonia, leiturgia, didache,* and *kerygma*.

Every preacher and storyteller knows that there is more power in showing than in telling. Sermon imagery gives listeners something to see with their ears. This kind of seeing may not always lead to believing, but it certainly offers the hearer an experience of that which is being imaged in a way beyond that achieved by simply telling about the same dynamic or concern. But we must be careful what kind of experience we are trying to create. We do not only want to offer straight hearers an experience in which they "see" homosexuals as acceptable "others" in the church. While we preachers want this effect, it is not enough. We need to include homosexuals in images of the church in ways that heterosexual listeners *identify* with them as they experience the image. Such identification will break down barriers and create unity in ways prosaic discourse could never do.

In addition to imagery, it is worth adding one other sermon-specific strategy for preaching a nonheterosexist ecclesiology, and this one deals with range of content. No sermon should try to deal with the whole of ecclesiology, with all four of the marks and/or all five of the practices of the church. Forcing too much onto a congregation in a single sermon will lead to kerygmatic indigestion. This is the case if you are just trying to present ecclesiology to the church in general. It is even more the case if you are trying to present the church re-visioned in ways the congregation has not before considered.

On the other hand, there is a great deal of overlap in the significance of the marks and in how the practices manifest those marks. One and catholic (unity in diversity and mutuality), after all, are very closely related concepts, even though we distinguish between them. Thus dealing with one of the marks of the church in a sermon will often necessitate corralling others in as well. We just need to keep the corral from growing too large if congregants are going to be able to be claimed by the ecclesiological message we offer.

Sample Sermon: "I Believe in the [cough] Church"

THE FOLLOWING SERMON DEALS with the marks of the church as unity in diversity but does so through the lens of mutuality. The Scripture text for the sermon is Philippians 2:1–13, the epistle lection for Proper 21 in Year A of the Revised Common Lectionary. Embedded in this passage is the Christ hymn that has been influential in including the idea of *kenosis* (emptying) into Christology and soteriology. This pre-Pauline liturgical piece is worthy of homiletical attention in its own right, but Paul uses the hymn (like any good preacher who quotes a hymn in a sermon!) to address a specific situation of conflict—in this case, in the church at Philippi.

Paul's response to this conflict is a timely word for the caustic tone of conflict that rages in the church today (as it so often has throughout the history of the church). The sermon was written to address such conflict and not heterosexism specifically. But the climactic image at the end of the sermon presents the question of homosexuality in the church as an example of the conflict ongoing in the church in relation to issues of sexual orientation. The image attempts to *show* how the church is the unified-in-diversity church in growing through a dialogue characterized by mutuality instead of a debate in which one side defeats the other. In the process of offering the congregation an experience of the broad focus on conflict, the listeners also experience themselves as a church in the process of moving beyond heterosexism.

Philippians 2:1–13

[1] *If then there is any encouragement in Christ, any consolation from love, any sharing in the Spirit, any compassion and sympathy,* [2] *make my joy complete: be of the same mind, having the same love, being in full accord and of one mind.* [3] *Do nothing from selfish ambition or conceit, but in humility regard others as better than yourselves.* [4] *Let each of you look not to your own interests, but to the interests of others.* [5] *Let the same mind be in you that was in Christ Jesus,*

⁶ *who, though he was in the form of God,*
    did not regard equality with God
    as something to be exploited,
⁷ *but emptied himself,*
    taking the form of a slave,
    being born in human likeness.
And being found in human form,
    ⁸ *he humbled himself*
    and became obedient to the point of death—
    even death on a cross.
⁹ *Therefore God also highly exalted him*
    and gave him the name
    that is above every name,
¹⁰ *so that at the name of Jesus*
    every knee should bend,
    in heaven and on earth and under the earth,
¹¹ *and every tongue should confess*
    that Jesus Christ is Lord,
    to the glory of God the Father.

¹² *Therefore, my beloved, just as you have always obeyed me, not only in my presence, but much more now in my absence, work out your own salvation with fear and trembling;* ¹³ *for it is God who is at work in you, enabling you both to will and to work for his good pleasure.*

I Believe in the [cough] Church

I remember once, in a group discussion of the Nicene Creed, someone saying: "Do you have a hard time reciting the Creed when you get to the last part where you have to profess faith in the church? We start off by saying that we believe in God as Creator, in Christ as Savior, and in the Holy Spirit. Then, without taking a breath, we move right on to the church. Do you have the same faith in the church that you have in God? Anyone who has ever served on a church committee must surely get a catch in their throat when they get to that part of the Creed? 'I believe in the one [cough], holy, [cough], catholic [cough], and apostolic church.'"

He's right, you know. I mean, think about it: this is the church that started with a small band of men and women who faithfully followed Jesus, and as it grew and moved across the planet, it split more times than all the paramecium of the universe. Across two millennia, we have fought about and divided over the Trinity, what books should be included in the Bible, the date on which we should celebrate Easter, whether the Bible could be translated into languages that laity could read, the number of sacraments, the nature of the sacraments, the nature of original sin, indulgences, ecclesiastical hierarchy, divorce, religious experience, slavery, evolution, the ordination of women, and the use of organ music in worship. "I believe in the one [cough], holy [cough], catholic [cough] church."

Of course, the beat goes on . . . all the battles of the church are not in the past. And, let's be clear: "the church" that is still fighting and divided today is not just some little segment of the church. I'm choking on the church universal. Every denomination has its share of scandals, and backbiting, and schism between the left and right. I mean, fill a room with all of the churches of the world, put on a blindfold, turn around three times, and you still couldn't miss putting a tail on a donkey if you wanted to. Turn this way and you stick the infallibility of Scripture. Over here, you hit child sexual abuse. There, plagiarism in the pulpit. Oops, there goes prayer in schools. That way, that way, and that way gets you the role of women in church leadership. Aim at any of those on that side of the room and you'll hit the division between the first-world and the third-world church. Yikes, hit any number over here and you get the issue of abortion. Stop almost anywhere and you'll stick a tail in a church fighting wars over music styles. And spin around fast jabbing over and over again and you'll hit debate after debate about sexual orientation. We are a church in disarray. "I believe in [cough] the one [cough], holy [cough], catholic [cough] church."

It's hard to have faith in the church when it looks like this. I don't mean to imply that some of these arguments aren't concerned with very important issues. They are, and the stakes for the church are significantly high. The stakes are never small when you are struggling with how best to be faithful to God. It's not the content of the debates that bothers me so much as it is the *manner* in which the church debates them. We may not throw each other out of balconies as they did in the early church when they were debating the divinity of Christ, but we are quite willing to throw each other out of the church, at least out of "our" church. We may call all Christians our "sisters and brothers," but we don't have to look far past the last election to be faced with the reality that those within the church who disagree with each other's views treat each other as opponents, as enemies, as combatants. We, whoever "we" are, consider them, whoever "they" are, less Christian than us. We are a church marred by deep conflict. "I believe in [cough] the one[cough], catholic [cough] church."

But not only is this not something new, in some sense this is the way it has been since the beginning of Christianity, since that small band of followers first began proclaiming Christ to the world. Our earliest documents in the New Testament come from Paul, and his letters are filled with church strife. Now to be sure he has caused his share of strife and is, to this day, quoted in support of this side or that of church battles. But in a number of letters his chief reason for corresponding with the congregation was to address conflict in the church. Take, for example, First Corinthians. No denomination has ever been more divided than the collection of house churches in Corinth. In First Corinthians, Paul has to deal with divisions over who was baptized by whom, sexual immorality, lawsuits between fellow Christians, food offered to idols, practices at the Lord's Supper, speaking in tongues in worship, whether women should speak in church at all, and the bodily resurrection of the dead. Or take Galatians. The Christians in Galatia aren't divided over a flock of different issues like those in Corinth, but the one question that troubles them divides them all the more deeply: To become fully Christian must you first become fully Jewish? Paul solves the issue by answering without blinking, "No." Paul writes numerous letters to deal with church conflict all over the ancient Roman Empire.

But . . . Paul doesn't write the letter to the church in Philippi to deal with conflict. Paul is in prison and facing trial. So the Philippian church had been praying for him and sent him a care package, delivered by Epaphroditus. While visiting Paul, Epaphroditus became ill. But when he recovered, Paul sent him back with the letter to thank the church for its support. It's that simple: his parents trained him well to write thank you notes when he received a gift, and Philippians is a thank you note.

But even when saying thank you, Paul just can't resist doing a little conflict management. He's so used to doing it in all of the other letters that he just can't help throwing it in here, too. Without even really naming a specific issue he does reference some bickering in the church. So Paul describes an ethic for being the church. It's beautiful in its simplicity. It's astounding in its depth. He says, "Be of the same mind." Be of the same mind. Now that sounds like he's saying that Christians should agree on everything, but

I think something is at stake here that is more significant than intellectual assent. "Be of the same mind," he says, but then without taking a breath, he goes on to clarify what that means, "Let the same mind be in you that was in Christ Jesus." It is not that we have to agree with one another 100 percent. It is that we should give 110 percent in trying to treat one another in accordance with the character of Christ.

In case they didn't quite get it, Paul reminds the Philippians what the character of Christ is, so that they will know exactly how they are to be in community with sisters and brothers of the faith. He does so with a technique that every hackneyed preacher uses here and there in the pulpit—he quotes a hymn. I don't know how big the Christian hymnal would have been twenty or so years after Jesus' crucifixion, but I assume Paul is quoting a hymn the Philippians already knew—like me ending this sermon with "Amazing Grace" or "O For a Thousand Tongues to Sing" or "Let Us Break Bread Together." Anyway, this is the way the first verse of the hymn that Paul quotes goes:

> Let the same mind be in you that was in Christ Jesus,
> who, though he was in the form of God,
>> did not regard equality with God
>> as something to be exploited,
> but emptied himself,
>> taking the form of a slave,
>> being born in human likeness.
> And being found in human form,
>> he humbled himself
>> and became obedient to the point of death—
>>> even death on a cross.

Paul goes on to quote the second verse of the hymn that deals with the exaltation of Christ—because, you know, preachers don't think there can be too much of a good thing when it comes to quoting hymns—but it's this first verse, this image of Christ as self-emptying and self-humbling, that Paul offers as the basis of a church ethic. We Christians may fervently disagree about abortion, the ordination of women, homosexuality, whether salvation is only for Christians, whether once you are saved you are always saved, and whether the Ten Commandments ought to be displayed in courthouses across the land. But in the midst of debating these issues, we should be emptying ourselves, humbling ourselves, for those with whom we are fervently arguing. "Be of the same mind." "Let the same mind be in you that was in Christ Jesus."

There's a church I know that had as part of its mission statement to "welcome all." This was a simple enough goal until the community around the church changed. Until society changed. So the question arose for the church, "What do we really mean by 'all'?" Does that "all" cross over economic boundaries? Does it cross out racial differences? What do people of the cross do when people of different sexual orientations begin knocking on the door? So they began talking about it. They began arguing about i. They became divided by it. Divided by "all." Something had to change or all that would be left would be to divide up the spoils.

So they did something simple, something deep. They sort of listened to Paul. They scheduled another conversation to talk about this "all," but when people arrived for the debate, there in the center of the room, waiting for them, was a loaf of bread and a cup of juice. There it stood waiting until after the conversation to be shared. Waiting for Communion. Waiting and saying, "Let the same mind be in you that was in Christ Jesus, whose death we remember in this meal."

And the conversation was different this time. In one circle, for instance, there were two men—one younger, one older—who were at an impasse over how the church should respond to homosexuals. This was especially problematic for the younger one, because he *was* gay. But there with that bread and that chalice in the middle of the room, he laid aside his assumption that the older man hated him and feared him. He emptied himself of that and opened himself to learning that the older man cared deeply about fidelity to Scripture and just couldn't figure out how to read the Bible differently. And the older, heterosexual man, too—with the body and blood sitting right there in front of him—humbled himself and listened to the younger man's story about what it is like to be a gay man trying to live out the Christian faith. At the end of the conversation—and this time it was a conversation and not a debate—those two men still had some disagreements between them. But now they were able to stand side by side to receive Communion. They were able to stand side by side in Communion with one another. One was able to hand the bread to the other and say, "This is the body of Christ, *given for you.*" And the other was able to pass the cup to the first and say, "This is the blood of Christ, *given for you.*"

In the background, can't you just hear, "Let us break bread together on our knees, let us break bread together . . ." OK, I won't quote a hymn.

How about quoting a creed instead? "I believe in the one [cough], holy [cough], catholic [cough], and apostolic church." No, wait, wait: I can do better than that. [Clear throat.] "I believe in the one, holy, catholic, and apostolic church."

3

Gay Rights

WALKING INTO THE FELLOWSHIP hall after the first service, you overhear Stan and Will, a couple now for two years, talking to Lissa and Ruth. You know that Stan and Will have been keeping separate homes but are now ready to take the next step in their relationship to give up their individual apartments and move into a larger one together. Lissa and Ruth are staples in the gay community and have lived together and reared children together for the last twenty-five years. What you hear troubles you: Stan wants to know how long it took Lissa and Ruth to find a house, because he and Stan have just lost out on the fourth apartment they tried to lease, and he has the feeling it was because they are gay. He cannot prove it, of course, because every manager has given a different reason for refusing to rent to them, but without there being any civil protections in place in your city, he and Will know that it is still legal to discriminate in housing based on sexual orientation. Their next step, he tells Ruth, is for Stan to go and apply for an apartment by himself and then take on Will as a "roommate." Lying like this about their relationship hurts both of them and has put a strain on their relationship, as Will hates the idea of going back in the closet because of homophobic real estate managers. Still, more than anything, they want to live together.

The brief conversation reminds you that for all the strides society has made in accepting homosexuals, the struggle continues in large and small ways—from international laws persecuting gays and lesbians, to your state's stand on gay marriage, to your city's fair housing ordinances, to your denomination's stand on leadership for gays and lesbians. At this point, you find that you are fed up with the large and small indignities your homosexual congregants must face. It is time to address in the pulpit this oppressive use of political power to take away the rights, to take away the personhood, of gay citizens. However, while gay church members will feel supported because their situations have been named in the context of the gospel, some people in the pews will say you are stepping over the line of church and state. Some straight allies will cheer, but other parishioners will say the pulpit is the place to address spiritual issues, not political ones. What are you to say—and how are you to say it—if you are going to get the whole assembly to engage the issue in a healthy manner and not simply rile some and pander to others? How do you preach the gospel in a prophetic manner that addresses this public issue while being a pastor to all?

THE CHURCH AND CIVIL RIGHTS

Hesed is not only a characteristic of God—the image of God imprinted on us that distinguishes us from the rest of creation—it is also an ethic of the communal church. And as such an ethic, *hesed* involves not only inner-communal behavior (as the concept was used in the previous chapter on ecclesiology) but communal behavior oriented toward the public sphere. The command to love our neighbor as ourselves is more than a personal way of treating individuals. It drives the institutional church's engagement in political matters. As Cornel West is often quoted as saying, "Never forget that justice is what love looks like in public."[1] Or as Martin Luther King Jr., asserted,

> Power without love is reckless and abusive, and love without power is sentimental and anemic. Power at its best is love implementing the demands of justice, and *justice at its best is power correcting everything that stands against love.*[2]

As an institution the church has always claimed a vocational identity of being a community of love struggling for justice in the world (even during the many times it has failed to live up to its calling). This identity is rooted in the idea that the church is an extension of the *missio Dei,* God's salvific

1. In the film *Call + Response*, directed by Justin Dillon, 2008, Fair Trade Pictures.

2. Martin Luther King Jr., "Where Do We Go from Here?" delivered at the eleventh Annual SCLC Convention, Atlanta, August, 16, 1967 (emphasis added), http://mlk-kppo1.stanford.edu/index.php/encyclopedia/documentsentry/where_do_we_go_from_here_delivered_at_the_11th_annual_sclc_convention/.

will in and for the world (see Chapter 2). As the extension of God's salvation, the church is first called to name and address sin as that *from which* we must be saved. Human brokenness manifests itself in many different ways, from the personal to the structural. Much of the work the church does and should focus on is brokenness at the individual or relational level. However, when the church addresses an issue of injustice, it is attempting to bring God's salvation to bear on systemic or structural sins, that is, brokenness in human relationships that has become so entrenched that lack of love for neighbor is woven into the very fabric of society in forms like sexism, racism, classicism, and heterosexism.

In its life, the church repents (or needs to repent) of those times when it either failed to stand up against structural sin or, worse, perpetuated it itself. But we celebrate those times when we have allowed God to work through us to stand on the side of right, when God moved society toward more just treatment of those who have suffered oppression. These two actions can happen simultaneously in majority congregations and denominations: e.g., the white church repents of the ways it allowed, participated in, and profited from racism in the past while working to combat it in the present; or churches dominated by male leadership confess their past patriarchy as they strive to provide and benefit from equal opportunities for women in the structures of Christian leadership.

Now the church is at the point—or better, is long past the point—in its history where it can and should repent of the numerous ways in which it is has provided theological underpinnings for society's heteronormativity, heterosexism, and homophobia. It should be at the place to focus its energies on joining the struggle for civil rights for homosexuals. While such struggle will require social action of the church that moves beyond the homiletical focus of this book, such action cannot be effective without the issue of gay rights being included in the proclamation of God's good news. For instance, by preaching that all humans (not simply heterosexuals) are created in God's image in their ability to embrace and act of out God's *hesed* (as described in Chapter 1) and that the theological description of marriage used in heterosexual weddings today applies just as easily to gay weddings and unions (Chapter 4), we are already working to dismantle any rhetoric that claims gays are seeking "special rights" instead of "equal rights."[3]

3. The rhetorical strategy of labeling gay rights as "special" rights is intended to characterize gays and lesbians as asking for rights that heterosexuals do not enjoy—as asking to be *privileged over* heterosexuals. This is misleading and damaging rhetoric, however. In asking to be listed in the fair housing statutes, for instance, homosexuals are simply

There are times, though, when a broad theological approach is not enough. There are times when preachers should and will feel called to take on specific issues of civil rights for homosexuals because of something derogatory said about a gay person in the congregation, an incident in the local high school where a gay teen was bullied, local legislation that does not provide equal protections in housing as described above, a state bill being proposed to ban gay marriage, a change in policy concerning homosexuals in the military, or a gay activist executed in a country where it is illegal to be gay.

This list of examples of specific issues of gay rights necessitates that we pause to note the challenges to writing (and reading/using) this chapter. The first is that in different geographical and cultural contexts, the civil rights issues affecting the lives and well-being of homosexuals will be different. How a gay person or couple feels in terms of self-worth and safety at work, attending church, sitting in a restaurant, or walking down the street is very different in states that ban gay marriage versus those that have been forced to accept gay marriage by the courts and those that have passed a laws explicitly affirming that gay couples have the right to marry. There are too many variables like this for us to address in a single volume, much less a single chapter. Readers will have to be in conversation with the principles and strategies we suggest and choose from among them and adapt them as appropriate for their particular situations.

---

asking for a *correction* to homophobic practices of discrimination in housing and not for a unique right that heterosexuals do not have. Such rights level the playing field rather than tipping it in favor of heterosexuals. Likewise in advocating for the right to marry, these rights simply correct a wrong and do not add benefits that homosexuals will reap over heterosexuals, or worse, that heterosexuals will lose if homosexuals are allowed to have them. Language of special rights is damaging rhetoric because it pits homosexuals against heterosexuals and it is meant to keep gays and lesbians as "other" than those who should claim all civil rights by suggesting that they/we believe they/we are more deserving of the protections and benefits of civil rights than heterosexuals.

It is further damaging because such rhetoric pits marginalized groups against one another in their common quest for equal protections under the law. Historically, many marginalized groups have not wanted to admit gays and lesbians into the common call for equal protection under the law because giving rights to homosexuals has been perceived as too divisive an issue in dominant culture and would lessen the chances that a minority group would gain the benefits it needs and deserves. Thus rights for homosexuals has been viewed as somehow "tainting" a general call for civil rights and the focus on gay civil rights has been perceived as a threat to civil rights for other minority groups. The rhetoric of special rights thus has the effect of suggesting that homosexuals want more than either heterosexuals in general or minority groups in particular have or should have.

A second challenge to writing or using this chapter is that the landscape concerning gay civil rights is changing rapidly, in both positive and negative ways. When we first began thinking about writing this book, DOMA (the federal Defense of Marriage Act) was still the law of the land. While we have been writing it, some states have acknowledged that gays have the right to marry while others have passed laws or constitutional amendments prohibiting or reinforcing prohibitions on gay marriage. As we have drawn the writing process to a close, a great deal of public focus has turned to the international stage with Russia's passage of a law banning propaganda of nontraditional sexual relationships in relation to the 2014 Winter Olympics and Uganda's passage of a law making homosexuality punishable with life in prison—the bill originally proposed execution—accompanied by tabloid efforts to out gays. By the time the publisher edits the book and the printer compiles it, the map will have been redrawn again. And by the time you pick up the book to read it, it may have been redrawn yet again. This type of flux in civil rights-related debate and activity is likely to be the status quo for a while. This means that while we are limited in what we can say at the moment of writing that will be directly applicable to coming scenarios, the need for preachers to speak of and to specific incidents and issues as they develop is all the more urgent.

Even though many legal lines in the sand will shift in the coming days until they are, hopefully, erased, the basic categories of gay rights at stake will remain the same, as will traces of social and ecclesial heterosexism and homophobia. Thus there is still work to do. In what follows, we examine the basic categories of civil and ecclesial rights issues of which preachers need to be aware so that they are better equipped to address specific incidents of discrimination when they arise.

CIVIL RIGHTS AT STAKE

A standard sort of description of what a civil right is and what is at stake in protecting such a right is offered on a website hosted by Cornell University Law School:

> A civil right is an enforceable right or privilege, which if interfered with by another gives rise to an action for injury. Discrimination occurs when the civil rights of an individual are denied or

interfered with because of their membership in a particular group or class.[4]

Denials of civil rights for homosexuals are of three broad types—economic, protective, and familial rights. The lines between these types are blurry and most of the examples we mention could fit under two of them or even under all three. Still, the delineation of these types is a helpful way to get a handle on the range of civil rights at stake when we think about how to address them in our sermons.

Economic Rights

Discrimination against gay persons and couples can result in unfair economic hardship not experienced by others in society. The most obvious expression of this form of discrimination is when an individual can be denied employment or can be fired on the basis of sexual orientation. While some states make such discrimination illegal, there is no federal law prohibiting it.[5]

In public discussion in the last two decades, the struggle against this form of oppression has focused especially on the military. Historically, homosexuals were not allowed to serve in the military. In 1993, Don't Ask, Don't Tell (DADT) became law. The intent was to keep the prohibition in place, but to discourage enforcement. In other words, closeted gays could serve and would not be forced out, but gay men or lesbians who were out of the closet would be discharged. In 2010 DADT was repealed, and a stream of advances for homosexual individuals and same-sex couples and families in military life have been part of the news cycle ever since.

While the military has made advances to be celebrated, there are other situations where employment discrimination continues to be a significant problem. One situation especially damning for gay men and lesbians is in relation to jobs working with children. Out of fear and hatred, homosexuals are often stereotyped as pedophiles and those who commit child sexual abuse. Even though this stereotype has long been debunked,[6] out

4. "Civil Rights: An Overview," Legal Information Institute, http://www.law.cornell.edu/wex/civil_rights.

5. See "Employment Non-Discrimination Act," Human Rights Campaign, http://www.hrc.org/laws-and-legislation/federal-legislation/employment-non-discrimination-act.

6. See, for instance, Gregory Herek, "Facts about Homosexuality and Child Molestation," http://psychology.ucdavis.edu/faculty_sites/rainbow/html/facts_molestation.html.

gay individuals are often not considered for positions as school teachers, coaches, or pediatricians.

In addition to employment issues, economic discrimination against homosexuals is manifested in the form of refusal to rent or sell a dwelling to a person that is out of the closet or same-sex couple. The Fair Housing Act (part of the Civil Rights Act of 1968) prohibited housing discrimination on the basis of race, color, religion, sex, or nation origin. In 1988 discrimination on the basis of disability and familial status was added.[7] There is still no federal protection in place to prohibit housing discrimination on the basis of sexual orientation.

Because households are, among other things, corporate economic entities, all of the familial issues discussed below have economic implications and could be included under this heading. The right to marry, for instance, includes the right to file taxes together, own property together, divide property justly in the case of divorce, and assume death benefits are provided for one's spouse. Excluding familial rights from part of the population on the basis of sexual orientation is a clear form of economic oppression.

Gay persons should have the right to pursue happiness in the form of economic well-being on the same plane as everyone else, and the church and its preachers should help establish the level playing field in the name of the God in whose image we are all created.

Right to Dignity

The use of "dignity" in contemporary discussions of equal rights can be anchored in the use of the term in The Universal Declaration of Human Rights, adopted by the United Nations in 1948.[8] The first article of the declaration reads,

> All human beings are born free and equal in dignity and rights. They are endowed with reason and conscience and should act towards one another in a spirit of brotherhood [*sic*].

While this language of the right to dignity can certainly apply to all human or civil rights, including economic and familial rights, here we are using

7. "Title VIII: Fair Housing and Equal Opportunity," at US Department of Housing and Urban Development, "http://portal.hud.gov/hudportal/HUD?src=/program_offices/fair_housing_equal_opp/progdesc/title8.

8. "The Universal Declaration of Human Rights," http://www.un.org/en/documents/udhr/.

the label to explore the narrower category in which every human being has the right to safety and inclusion in society as a valued member thereof. To borrow the language of Martin Buber, the right to dignity in this sense is the right to be treated as a "thou" instead of an "it" in public affairs.[9]

In terms of safety, homosexuals have the right to be protected from abusive speech and violent behavior. While all people have the right to free speech, including those who disagree with or even simply do not like gay people, this free speech should be respectful of the "other" who is gay. These people can argue against gay marriage but do not have the right to lie about, slander, bully, insult, or threaten gay people in the process of expressing their disagreement.

In addition to protection from hate speech of different sorts, homosexuals have the right to be protected from physical violence, especially violence directed at them for no other reason than that they are homosexual. Gay men should not be beaten and lesbians not made victims of "corrective rape."[10] Gay teens should not be pushed to suicide by cyberbullying. Hate crime laws are designed to deter such violence by increasing the penalties against those who perpetrate a violent crime on the basis of prejudice toward a specific target group. While the Civil Rights Acts of 1968 prohibited intimidation, threats, and violence on the basis of race, color, religion, or national origin, it was not until over forty years later, after the horrific and well-publicized death of Matthew Shepherd, that hate crime laws were extended to apply to attacks based on hatred of sexual orientation.[11]

Not all the cases of denying gay people their due dignity as human beings in public affairs are as graphic as those that call for protection from emotional or physical abuse that rises to the level of a hate crime. This category of injustice also occurs when businesses refuse to do business with a person or a couple on the basis of their sexual orientation (and especially when state governments consider ratifying such behavior legally). It occurs when social clubs or affinity groups refuse membership on the basis of sexual orientation. In relation to the scope of this book, an especially

---

9. Martin Buber, *I and Thou*, trans. Walter Kaufman (New York: Charles Scribner's Sons, 1970; originally published in 1923).

10. For example, see Clare Carter, "The Brutality of 'Corrective Rape,'" *New York Times*, July 27, 2013, http://www.nytimes.com/interactive/2013/07/26/opinion/26corrective-rape.html.

11. See "Matthew Shepard and James Byrd, Jr., Hate Crimes Prevention Acts of 2009," The United States Department of Justice, http://www.justice.gov/crt/about/crm/matthewshepard.php.

troubling example of this one is mentioned in the previous chapter, the Boy Scouts of America. Until recently the organization neither allowed gay boys to join as members nor gay men to serve as troop leaders. Even though the former prohibition has been recently dropped, the latter one remains in place (see the discussion of homosexuals being restricted from working with young children above). The reason this particular example is troubling in the context of this book's focus on preaching is that so many scout troops are located in and/or sponsored by churches, including progressive churches struggling to overcome heterosexism.

Gay persons should have the right to pursue happiness in the form of being treated as a person with inherent dignity on the same plane as everyone else, and the church and its preachers should help establish the level playing field in the name of the God in whose image we are all created.

Familial Rights

Human Rights Education Associates has the following on their website:

> The family is the fundamental and natural unit of society and requires the full protection of the state. Human rights law upholds the positive right of all peoples to marry and found a family. It upholds the ideal of equal and consenting marriage and tries to guard against abuses which undermine these principles. It is not prescriptive as to the types of families and marriages that are acceptable, recognizing tacitly that there are many different forms of social arrangements around the world. . . .[12]

The last sentence of the quote clarifying that human rights affirmation of the family has avoided prescribing particular familial arrangements implies that family structures involving gay couples can and should be protected as a right as much as those involving heterosexual couples, single parents, and so forth. But as the web page indicates, this is not universally recognized:

> Whether these rights apply to same-sex couples has become a matter of discussion in recent times. Although human rights law does not make explicit reference to this, a number of its provisions concerning the right to marry and have a family, right to equality and non-discrimination etc. can be interpreted to mean that gay

12. "The Right to Family," Human Rights Education Associates, http://www.hrea.org/index.php?base_id=158.

and lesbian couples should enjoy the protection of human rights law.[13]

The church needs to argue from the pulpit that withholding familial rights from homosexuals is an unjustified act of prejudice and a hindrance to human reception and manifestation of God's *hesed*.

The most obvious and most discussed form of familial discrimination is the refusal of the right to marry on the basis of sexual orientation. As highlighted above this act of discrimination has serious economic ramifications, but it also hinders gay persons in achieving the level of emotional, spiritual, and relational stability that is a goal of marriage. Human beings seek to create commitments that last a lifetime. To deny homosexuals the right to such commitment and then to condemn them for being promiscuous is a double standard of the most egregious sort.

The denial of the right to marry carries with it numerous other forms of discrimination. Under the heading of Economic Rights above, we already mentioned the loss of financial protection in the case of divorce or the death of a partner. Perhaps, though, one of the most painful ramifications of this form of discrimination is the manner in which homosexuals are denied access to their partners and to decision-making processes in the case of the emergency hospitalization of their partners. In most states, even if domestic partnerships are recognized, gay couples must have set up power of attorney agreements in advance for this to occur.

The restriction of familial rights for gay men and lesbians also affects their ability to have, provide foster care for, adopt, and raise children. Even though society has made great strides in moving beyond accepting only the traditional heterosexual nuclear family in that it accepts single-parented (heterosexual) families, much prejudice still exists around accepting gay (single or coupled) parents. Stereotypes and misinformation are rampant in this debate: children raised by gay parents will be molested (see earlier discussion), will be harassed, will become gay (assuming this is a bad thing), and will develop psychological problems. Studies show that all of these claims except one are false. The one that is true is that children of gay parents are teased and harassed during adolescence. This, however, is not a problem internal to the family or due to the lack of parenting abilities of gay adults. It is due to the way children of straight parents learn to deny the dignity of homosexuals and anyone related to and accepting of homosexuals.[14]

13. Ibid.

14. For a short argument against these stereotypes in relation to gay men and lesbians

In other words, the harassment is an argument for the need for the familial rights of homosexuals to be affirmed and enforced, not a reason for them to be denied.

Gay persons should have the right to pursue happiness in the form of marrying and creating families on the same plane as everyone else, and the church and its preachers should help establish the level playing field in the name of the God in whose image we are all created.

ECCLESIAL RIGHTS AT STAKE

Even as the church works to remove the speck from society's eye, it must remove the log from its own. The church has not stood idly by while society has discriminated against homosexuals. Unfortunately, the church has been an active partner, and often a leader, in this discrimination. It should embarrass those of us in the church that the military is more progressive than the body of Christ in the struggle to overcome the oppression of homosexuals. We must repent of our attitudes and actions of the past (and present) and change our course for the future.

Of course, such positive change is occurring in pockets of ecclesial life. Some denominations, regional judicatories, and individual congregations have instituted policies affirming gay rights. In communions where those rights are still suppressed, clergy and laity are acting out in forms of ecclesial disobedience (e.g., by performing same-sex unions and weddings that are prohibited by church law) in order to reveal the injustice.

Still, other individuals and organized groups within "mainline" denominations lash out and actively strive to pull the church in the reverse direction. Thus progressive pastors cannot take recent advances for granted and assume the church will "naturally" move toward the full inclusion of homosexuals if we simply allow it to do so. We must continue to speak as prophets, holding the church accountable and calling it to lean toward God's just reign. There are three areas of church life that continue to need to be addressed if the church is to embrace its identity as a nonheterosexist institution working for the *missio Dei*—the right to be married in and by the church, the right to church membership, and the right to assume roles of leadership in the church. The chapter on ecclesiology (Chapter 2)

seeking to adopt, see "Gay and Lesbian Adoptive Parents: Resources for Professionals and Parents: Issues and Concerns," Child Welfare Information Gateway, https://www.childwelfare.gov/pubs/f_gay/f_gayb.cfm.

touches on these from a different perspective, allowing us to name them here without requiring too much exposition.

The Right to Church Weddings

Because we have discussed the secular side of this issue above and devote the next chapter to preaching at weddings and union ceremonies, we need not spend much time here exploring the issue of same-sex marriage. Still, we should name explicitly that we cannot fight for the secular right for homosexuals to marry and establish families and not lead the way in the church by performing weddings for homosexual couples. Whatever standards we hold for allowing heterosexual couples to be married by the church—for instance, church membership, profession of Christian faith, or premarital counseling—should be the same standards we hold for same-sex couples. Sexual orientation should not be a standard used to determine whether the church will name a union as created and blessed by God.

Gay persons should have the right to have their faith affirmed in the form of being married in the church just like everyone else, and preachers should help establish a level playing field in the name of the God in whose image we are all created.

The Right to Church Membership

While many conservative churches deny membership to homosexuals, most "mainline" churches accept gay members. This acceptance, however, is often a religious version of Don't Ask, Don't Tell. We force gay Christians into the closet in the sense that they are accepted so long as they do not make "gay issues" an issue for the church. As we illustrated in Chapter 2, gay couples are often accepted as long as they appear heterosexual. Worse is the attitude that we accept them as members because we "hate the sin but love the sinner." In other words, we let them into the church as sinners to save them from their sin of homosexuality.

Since all humans are created in God's image and since in baptism divisions between us are broken down (Gal 3:27–28), the church needs not only to accept gay members (i.e., tolerate those who seek a congregation out) but to invite and welcome gay Christians into the fold, and preachers should establish this attitude and mind set within their congregations in the name of the God in whose image we are all created.

The Right to Serve as Leaders

If gay Christians are to be embraced as full members of the church, they must be included in its leadership. The ministry of the baptized is not the ministry of the straight. The priesthood of all believers is not the priesthood of all heterosexuals. To allow homosexual Christians to be church members but not church leaders is to be open but not affirming.

If qualified gay laypersons are not invited to serve as Sunday School teachers, committee and board members, deacons, elders, liturgists, and representatives to denominational judicatories, we are cheating both those we are excluding and the church. Lesbians and gay men excluded from leadership are robbed of the chance to fulfill their calling as Christians and to find satisfaction in cooperating with their sisters and brothers to advance the mission of the church. The church is denied the unique gifts that any individual gay member—unique gifts because the person is a unique individual, not because she or he is gay—may bring to the work of the church. The church loses the chance to expand the diversity of experiences and outlooks in its leadership teams.

This right to serve must include the right to be ordained. While many "mainline" denominations and congregations accept homosexuals as members, and some invite gay men and lesbians to serve as lay leaders, few allow—much less encourage—them to become clergy. Until qualified gay Christians are invited to study for and enter the ministry, they will never be equal members in the body of Christ any more than African Americans or women were before they were admitted to the ordained ministry. Gay Christians need representatives standing in the pulpit and at the table.

Perhaps more importantly, once gay clergy stand to proclaim God's word and to give thanks over the bread and cup, they will be seen as representative of *all* Christians. Ordained ministry is a specialized and representative ministry of all who are baptized into the ministry of the church. When across the ecumenical landscape homosexual men and women can regularly be seen as representing the community of faith as a whole instead of representing only the gay community, the church will have finally overcome the structural sin of its internal heterosexism. Preachers must use the authority and power that accompanies stepping into the pulpit in order to help establish a level playing field for gays in church leadership in the name of the God in whose image we are all created.

HOMILETICAL STRATEGIES

Longitudinal Strategies

There are two primary strategies that pastors should employ across their preaching ministry year after year in relation to civil and ecclesial rights for homosexuals. These two strategies are opposite sides of the same coin.

The first is that preachers should regularly name issues of discrimination against gays as a group as part of their imagery in sermons when they are discussing structural or systemic sin. Telling stories of such discrimination alongside illustrations related to a range of other forms of oppression will lead hearers, especially heterosexual hearers, to recognize that heterosexist discrimination should concern the church at the same level these other, more commonly named forms of oppression concern us.

The second strategy is that preachers should regularly name advances and victories in the struggles against heterosexism as part of the imagery of the good news of the sermon, as part of giving flesh to God's salvific and providential care in the world. Especially important in this sense is to celebrate ways the church, and particularly the preacher's local congregation, has made strides in overcoming heterosexism. Even if the congregation continues to uphold some heterosexist practices and attitudes, celebrating small steps that have been taken as participating in God's mission will inspire other similar, even larger, steps to be taken rather than making hearers feel guilty or defensive. In common parlance, positive reinforcement in preaching is usually more effective than negative reinforcement in inspiring change. Moreover, while heterosexuals will be inspired to continue to make changes, homosexual hearers will have their lives validated in public ways before the congregation as a whole. Such validation makes great strides in eliminating the sense of tacit condemnation at worst or simple invisibility at best that homosexuals may feel in the wider church. Naming these two strategies in tandem—regularly using both discrimination against homosexuals and improvements in the area of gay rights as sermonic imagery—invites further conversation about heterosexism and sermonic structure.

All sermons move from an itch to a scratch, from a problem, puzzle, or concern of some sort to a resolution or answer. In other words, all sermons move from bad news to good news.[15] We preachers are quite good at

15. The language of "an itch to scratch" comes from Eugene L. Lowry, *The Homiletical Plot: The Sermon as Narrative Art Form* (Louisville: Westminster John Knox, 2001), 15–21; for use of this movement in diverse sermonic forms, see O. Wesley Allen Jr.,

showing the bad news, but too often we only tell the good news.[16] If preachers only show issues of heterosexism in the itch part of sermons while failing to show increasing rights for gays in the scratch, over time hearers will
experience every mention of issues related to the lives and well-being of
gay members of society and of our church (even advances in gay rights) as
bad news.

Sermon-Specific Strategies

The above longitudinal strategies are not enough when it comes to dealing
with gay rights. They, however, set a tone over time that allows preachers to
denounce incidents of prejudice, discrimination, and violence when they
occur and to celebrate specific victories in the struggle for gay rights when
they are achieved. When newscasts, blogs, and congregational talk are filled
with discussion about a church trial of a pastor who officiated at a same-sex
wedding or about a federal court striking down a law defining marriage
as only being between a man and a woman, the pulpit should not be the
only place where it is *not* discussed. Congregations long for their pastors
to address the real world in real time from the perspective of the faith that
stretches over eons.

This means that, at times, preachers will need to include a recent news
item dealing with an incident involving gay rights and will need to address
the issue explicitly as the focus of the sermon. A church trial in another
denomination in another part of the country might only call for a passing
reference in a sermon; but that same trial in one's own geographical and
denominational context needs to be addressed directly. Bullying named in
the news that led to a gay student switching high schools versus an incident
in which the bullying turned violent, putting a gay youth in the hospital
and a straight youth in jail, calls for different levels of explicitness in the
sermon. The level of immediacy and emotional impact an incident of either
discrimination against or victory for gay persons and gay rights has (or
should have) on a congregation determines the level of focused attention
we give it in a sermon.

To approach heterosexism in the head-on manner that dealing with
issues of civil rights and specific incidents involving civil rights demands

---

Determining the Form, Elements of Preaching (Minneapolis: Fortress, 2008), esp. 9–11.

16. See David L. Bartlett, "Showing Mercy," in ed. Mike Graves, *What's the Matter
with Preaching Today* (Louisville: Westminster John Knox, 2004), 23–26.

can lead preachers to make a fatal error in dealing with oppressors in these situations. In our zeal for rights for homosexuals, we can easily demonize those who have brought hardship and violence on gay men and lesbians. There are two reasons we must not do this. The first is theological: the oppressor is a victim of sin, just as the oppressed are. In fighting against heterosexism, we seek to offer God's liberation and salvation to both the victim and the victimizer. As Martin Luther King Jr. put it,

> There will come a time, in many instances, when the person who hates you most, the person who has misused you most . . . when you will have an opportunity to defeat that person. . . . That's the time you must not do it. That is the meaning of love. In the final analysis, love is not this sentimental something that we talk about. It's not merely an emotional something. Love is creative, understanding goodwill for all men [*sic*]. It is the refusal to defeat any individual. When you rise to the level of love, of its great beauty and power, you seek only to defeat evil systems. Individuals who happen to be caught up in that system, you love, but you seek to defeat the system.[17]

The second reason we should not demonize the oppressors is that there are people in our pews who identify with them. They likely do not agree that a gay person should be bullied, but they may still be trapped in the idea that homosexuality is a sin. By unsympathetically condemning the oppressor in a sermon illustration, the person in the pew may feel pushed away instead of invited to move ahead with us in overcoming heterosexist structures in society and in the church. We want to convert, not condemn, them. To preach prophetically and pastorally at the same time, we must not condone and make excuses for heterosexist or homophobic thinking or behavior, but neither must we damn those who think and behave in such ways to hell without parole. Instead we must guide hearers on a path out of the world of heteronormativity, both for their own good and for the good of the church and the world. Using imagery of straight persons and communities who have moved from aligning with oppression to standing in solidarity with the gay community in fighting for equal rights is one way of doing this.

17. Martin Luther King Jr., "Love Your Enemies," sermon delivered at Dexter Avenue Baptist Church, Montgomery, Alabama, November 17, 1957, http://mlk-kpp01.stanford.edu/index.php/encyclopedia/documentsentry/doc_loving_your_enemies/.

Sample Sermon: *"Yet"*

THE FOLLOWING SERMON IS based on Jeremiah 4:5–8, 23–28. The boundaries of the reading are a revision of the lesson from the Hebrew Bible for the Revised Common Lectionary early in September during Year C (Proper 19): Jeremiah 4:11–12, 22–28. The lection is composed of two excerpts from Jeremiah 4:5–31, a judgment oracle that makes readers want to turn their heads aside, for it displays the wrath of God with little covering of grace. The full oracle is too long a text (primarily containing poetry utilizing Hebraic parallelism) to be held in the ear in a liturgical setting, and so the RCL's decision to read only portions of the passage is a wise one. The RCL, however, does a poor job of choosing which portions should be read. Using vv. 11–12 to provide the context for the later portion of the oracle (instead of vv. 5–8 or at least vv. 5–6) does not help the hearers make sense of the reading when the phrase "at that time" in v. 11 refers back to the destruction coming from the north described in the opening of the oracle. Moreover, the primary RCL selection (vv. 22–28) does not follow the natural breaks in the passage. The sermon below followed a reading of Jeremiah 4:5–8, 23–28 and focused on it but always kept an eye on the fuller context of vv. 5–31.

In vv. 5–8, the imagery points to God bringing a violent military force from the north to destroy Zion. The foreign army is as close at hand as a lion that has already leaped out of hiding to attack its prey. In the rest of the oracle that follows, the destruction that is coming is imagined in a number of ways. In vv. 23–28, that destruction of Zion is described as total destruction, a reversal of the act of divine creation itself—the earth becomes waste/void, the heavens lose their light, the land becomes unstable, and life on land and in the air disappears.

In this context, v. 27 is a puzzle. It breaks out of poetry to speak in prose and to present a contradictory God. In the middle of the metaphors that present the judgment of Israel in terms of cosmic destruction, God says, "The whole land shall be a desolation; yet I will not make a full end." The shift in tone and style indicates that this line may be a later scribal addition to the original oracle. Regardless, in the overwhelming imagery of 4:5–31, v. 27 is a welcome sliver of hope.

The context for this sermon was that a new GLAAD (Gay & Lesbian Alliance Against Defamation) organization had formed on a local college campus at the beginning of the school year. This was the first organized group advocating for LGBT support and rights on the campus. It had been present at the student organization fair in mid August and had already held a few public events that gained it attention, both positive and negative. The negative attention had not risen to the level of gay bashing but looked like it could easily and quickly get there. The church for which this sermon was intended sat on the edge of campus. In the pews were students, staff, and faculty of the college, so the church had also been filled with talk about GLAAD's appearance on campus.

In one sense, the oracle's focus and tone invited the preacher to speak a word of judgment against those who were speaking negatively about GLAAD—as part of an effort to protect the student organization from those in the pew—then turn to speak negatively *to* the students in GLAAD. But the sliver of hope of v. 27 invited a different approach, of inviting hearers to imagine a different approach altogether.

JEREMIAH 4:5–8, 23–28

⁵ *Declare in Judah, and proclaim in Jerusalem, and say:*
Blow the trumpet through the land;
>*shout aloud and say,*
"Gather together, and let us go
>*into the fortified cities!"*
⁶ *Raise a standard toward Zion,*
>*flee for safety, do not delay,*
for I am bringing evil from the north,
>*and a great destruction.*
⁷ *A lion has gone up from its thicket,*
>*a destroyer of nations has set out;*
>*he has gone out from his place*
to make your land a waste;
>*your cities will be ruins*
>*without inhabitant.*
⁸ *Because of this put on sackcloth,*
>*lament and wail:*

"*The fierce anger of the* LORD
  has not turned away from us."

²³ *I looked on the earth, and lo, it was waste and void;*
  and to the heavens, and they had no light.
²⁴ *I looked on the mountains, and lo, they were quaking,*
  and all the hills moved to and fro.
²⁵ *I looked, and lo, there was no one at all,*
  and all the birds of the air had fled.
²⁶ *I looked, and lo, the fruitful land was a desert,*
  and all its cities were laid in ruins
  before the LORD, *before his fierce anger.*

²⁷ *For thus says the* LORD: *The whole land shall be a desolation; yet I*
will not make a full end.

²⁸ *Because of this the earth shall mourn,*
  and the heavens above grow black;
for I have spoken, I have purposed;
  I have not relented nor will I turn back.

YET

I like to think of myself as a social justice-oriented Christian. When I experience communities of faith that feed the hungry, that promote women in leadership roles, that invite in people of differing sexual orientations, that speak words of peace, that advocate for good stewardship of creation, and that pray for victims of oppressive violence, I believe I understand what the word "church" means. And although I am a North American, white male, I like to think that I have been shaped in some significant ways by voices in African American, feminist, womanist, and Latin American liberation theologies. And as a preacher I am drawn to those biblical texts that call us to care for the widow and the orphan, to those stories where Jesus crosses the borders of cultural propriety to touch and share meals with the unclean, and to those prophets who proclaim that God doesn't want empty ritual without practices of justice. I'm a Christian who values justice.

  The problem is that as a good, liberal Christian, I'm not a big fan of judgment. I like when Jesus says, "Blessed are the poor," but I want to quit reading before I get down to the part where he says, "Woe to the rich." I love that the Israelites are delivered from slavery, but I could do without the Egyptians losing their firstborn sons. Unlike Thomas Jefferson, if I had the chance to edit the Bible and remove the parts I didn't like, I wouldn't have worried about the miracle stories. Nope, I would've gotten rid of judgment. In my version of the Bible, God would have created a road map for the Israelites and the Canaanites to live together in harmony, Abraham would have been able to convince God to spare Sodom and Gomorrah, God would have given us the rainbow without the flood, and somehow God would have moved Adam and Eve out of the garden for their own growth as human beings instead of kicking them out with curses on the divine breath. I like justice, but I could do without judgment.

Which means I could do without a heck of a lot of the book of Jeremiah. Oh, the oracles that come from later in Jeremiah's ministry and show up late in the book of Jeremiah, when he offers hope to those living under Babylonian oppression—those parts I would keep. But in those oracles from earlier in his ministry—in the ones earlier in the book—he makes John the Baptist look like Shirley Temple. If I had been Jeremiah's editor, I would have taken out all that talk about the siege of Jerusalem, the razing of the temple, and the exile of the people; I would have taken out all those speeches where he says destruction will occur because God judges the people as unfaithful in their personal, religious, and social lives; I would have taken out all those oracles of retribution and judgment and tossed them in the shredder.

And that means that, were I Jeremiah's editor, the oracle in chapter 4 would definitely have to go. I mean, did you hear the language of judgment in today's reading? God is bringing evil from the north to affect divine wrath on Jerusalem. An empire's army is as ready to devour Israel as is a lion that has just leaped from the thicket toward its prey. The devastation of the land will be so overwhelming that it will seem that the work it took God six days to complete will be erased by a hot wind. The ordered earth will give way to the chaotic void. The sun and the moon and the stars will be extinguished. The tall, majestic mountains will curl up in a fetal position. Humanity will disappear. Birds of the air will flee. And the vegetation of the garden will become a desert. That's what the coming judgment will seem like. Earth will mourn and the heavens will become dark. I don't like judgment. If I were Jeremiah's editor, I would be hitting the delete button a lot on this oracle. But, lo, I am not the prophet's editor.

I am happy to report, however, that he did have one. Wiser than I, this editor didn't omit Jeremiah's words of judgment. Maybe the editor realized, with Jeremiah, that you can't have justice without judgment. The one implies the other. As one theologian has said, the judgment of God is that we must face the consequences of our actions.[18] God reconciles us to Godself, but that does not erase all the damage we have done to ourselves and to others. Our God is not a deus ex machina—a god of the machine in ancient Greek plays who soared down from the rafters in the last act to save the hero of the story. No, God judges us by granting us the freedom to pollute our water, to cheat on our spouse, to discriminate against those who are different and less powerful than we, to replace sacred worship with civil religion, to wear clothes made by American companies running sweatshops in Bangladesh. God judges us by granting us the freedom to gossip, to invade countries less powerful than we, to abuse our children, to scorn those whose skin is a different color. God judges us by granting us the freedom to open ourselves to the evil that will attack from the north, to turn the earth into a place of chaotic mourning. God judges us by forcing us to face the consequences of our actions. Jeremiah knew that justice doesn't make sense without judgment. And I guess his editor knew that as well, so the judgment of God stays in the text.

But the editor doesn't leave it at that. He recognizes that in the scheme of the book of Jeremiah as a whole, judgment gives way, or *leads* the way, to hope. But the editor refuses to make us wait for twenty-odd chapters to hear that message of hope. He doesn't take the judgment out. But claiming a small amount of scribal license, he slips just the tiniest hint of salvation in. Into the middle of Jeremiah's poetic oracle of judgment, this scribe inserts a line of prose:

> For thus says the Lord: The whole land shall be a desolation; yet I will not make a full end.

Oh, I love that word, "yet." It doesn't erase judgment and its consequences, but it does say that judgment is not the *final* word. Justice implies judgment, yes. But God's last word is: "yet I will not make a full end." When Paul Tillich asks how the prophets could speak such harsh words of judgment, his answer is that "beyond the sphere of destruction, they saw the sphere of

---

18. This line is recalled as being quoted from Reinhold Niebuhr, but we have been unable to find the quote itself.

salvation; because in the doom of the temporal, they saw the manifestation of the Eternal."[19] Yet.

The scribe left in all of Jeremiah's warnings of judgment, but added in a little bitty "yet I will not make a full end." True, this little prosaic insert into the oracle can't compare to the power of the imagery of destruction that surrounds it. In fact, if you read too quickly, you'll miss it. It's small. Only a dandelion in a junkyard. But there it is. Not fully interpreted. Not described in concrete imagery. Just mentioned in passing. Just hinted at. Just a reminder that when judgment is on center stage, and it is at times, salvation is peeking out through the slit in the curtain. We may not feel it as easily as we feel all the damage God allows us to wreak on ourselves and our neighbors, but we can catch a glimpse of hope that judgment is not a full end to us. It may even be a new beginning.

I guess it's a good thing that I'm not allowed to edit the Bible. But I sure am glad there was a scribe who took a little editorial license with Jeremiah. If that editor took the same license with some of my own memories of judgment, one would sound like this.

Every year in Atlanta, the gay pride parade is held on a Sunday in late June. The parade marches down one of the main thoroughfares of the city, which means it passes by some of the city's oldest churches. There is this one church that every year moved worship earlier so that its members could avoid having any contact with the homosexuals and the lesbians and the transvestites in the parade. Indeed, the women and children would be rushed home to get to safety. But some of the men would stay behind. They had two purposes. The first was to protect the church building from those in the parade. The second was to display signs proclaiming God's judgment on homosexuals, saying things like AIDS was sent by God.

Just across the street was a smaller, dying church that also dismissed worship early each year because of the parade. They did so for two reasons. First, they had to put up signs that proclaimed God's love for everyone. And second, they had to prepare trays of paper cups with ice water to give out to those in the parade to announce that all were welcome in their church. One year, an elderly woman who was handing out water decided to make a bold move. Instead of walking into the parade, she walked through it. She walked across the street to the men standing guard at the other church, and offered them a cup of water. All except one of them refused her gift

---

19. See Tillich's sermon on Jeremiah 4 and other oracles of judgment in *The Shaking of the Foundations* (New York: Charles Scribner's Sons, 1948), 1–11.

and tried to persuade her that God would judge those who welcomed such sinners.

And indeed God did. In fact God allowed both churches to suffer the consequences of their actions. Today, the guarded church building has been abandoned. Those who once worshiped there have fled to the suburbs and built their church there, but in reality it is little more than a country club with a chaplain. They do little to change individual lives and nothing to change the world. The water-giving church, on the other hand, has become one of the fastest-growing churches in Atlanta. Of course, its pews are filled with the likes of gays and lesbians, as well as homeless women and children from the shelter the church now sponsors. And they're filled with senior citizens and families with small children that don't know any better than to associate with such people. Oh, and one seat is always filled by the lone man from across the street who accepted the woman's gift of water that one hot, sunny day in June. "For thus says the Lord: The whole land shall be a desolation; yet I will not make a full end."

4

Weddings and Unions

You are the pastor of an open and affirming church in a state that doesn't recognize gay marriage. You have been proud of the stances that your congregation has taken on accepting gay members and on civil issues, including arguing for the right for gay marriage at the state level. You are in your office waiting for a gay congregant who has set an appointment to talk with you about a social issue. Mary walks in, with Fran, her partner. As soon as she begins speaking, you realize Mary has not come to discuss the legal issue of gay marriage. Instead, she and Fran have come to talk about it personally. They are tired of waiting on the state to change its laws and have decided they want to be married "in God's eyes"—whether the marriage is legal in the state's eyes or not. While you have been an advocate for gay marriage you have never actually been asked to officiate at a ceremony before. You immediately say "yes" to the request, congratulate them, and schedule premarital counseling sessions. The moment they leave your office, however, you begin to worry about what you are going to say at the ceremony.

THEOLOGY OF GAY MARRIAGE

Offering practical suggestions for preaching at the wedding or union ceremony of a gay couple is difficult because of two factors. The first factor is the rapidly changing landscape in relation to this topic. Public opinion polls show that whereas as little as five years ago a majority of the US population disapproved of homosexuals having the legal right to marry, the numbers are now reversed.[1] This legal right is indeed expanding, with an increasing minority of states approving domestic partnership and same-sex marriage laws, the Supreme Court's declaration of the Defense of Marriage Act's refusal of federal benefits to married gay couples to be unconstitutional, and the high court's dismissal of the case concerning California's Proposition 8 on procedural grounds, in effect making the law null and void. On the other hand, some conservative political and religious voices have grown louder in arguing against rights for gay couples, and a majority of states have passed statutes or constitutional amendments banning gay marriage and/or civil unions.

The second difficulty with offering practical advice for preaching at same-sex unions and weddings is that pastors reading this book come from different geographical regions with different laws and from different denominations with a wide range of theological and ecclesiastical stances related to homosexuality. For pastors at one end of the theological spectrum, preaching at a same-sex wedding or union ceremony would be celebrated within their tradition and by denominational powers, whereas for those at the other end of the spectrum it would be seen as an act of ecclesiastical disobedience that could result in the loss of credentials. The vast majority of pastors stand between these ends, in which their role at a gay wedding would likely result in receiving varied responses simultaneously.

One thing is clear in the midst of these sorts of transitions and complexities, however. Wherever different governing and denominational bodies land as this evolution continues, heteronormativity will remain the standard of culture in relation to marriage for some time. A pastor representing a denomination that values same-sex marriage and performing a gay wedding in a state that has legalized gay marriage will *still* be doing so in the face of significant levels of heterosexism throughout society.

Thus in this chapter, it is best to frame the question of preaching at a wedding or union ceremony for a gay couple in relation to the historical, theological context of weddings and marriage more than primarily in terms of the current dynamics in our cultural context.

In striving to examine the practice of preaching at a gay wedding or union ceremony in the context of heteronormative weddings and marriage,

---

1. See "Gay Marriage: Key Data Points from Pew Research," Pew Research Center, http://www.pewresearch.org/key-data-points/gay-marriage-key-data-points-from -pew-research/.

we propose neither to offer an exhaustive survey of the evolution of theology and practices of marriage in the church nor to argue for the appropriateness of gay marriage in light of tradition. The first task would be impossible in the scope of this work and the second task we simply assume to be the case. Instead our goal here is to offer a few glimpses into the historical background of weddings and marriage that will provide contemporary pastors who desire to preach at gay weddings language and concepts on which to draw.[2]

Our beginning point for thinking about these issues is to realize that the church has not always been involved in the business of marrying people. In the days of the early church in the Roman Empire, weddings were cultural, familial, legal ceremonies. Marriages might have been blessed by a representative of the church, but the ceremony itself was not performed by the church.

This Roman custom of having secular weddings followed the church into medieval Europe as well. Over time, however, priests became more involved in weddings. At first this was likely as much for logistical reasons as theological or liturgical ones. As one of the most educated persons in the village, the priest would be in charge of keeping some public records, including recording marriages. Thus couples would have their weddings outside the church building at the church door, with the priest serving as the witness and recorder of the event. This led to the priest blessing the union after the fact, having the couple (or wedding party as a whole) come into the church to receive the Eucharist to celebrate the wedding just accomplished, and perhaps blessing the marriage bed.

What should be clear here is that the church's role in the making of the marriage was secondary. A marriage in early medieval Europe was generally considered legal and binding if three requirements were met. First, consent to marry must be given. Neither the man nor the woman should be coerced into marriage. Given the patriarchy of the day, this consent often included the consent of the bride's father. Second, the marriage must be consummated sexually. And, third, the marriage must be enacted through cohabitation. As long as these three requirements had been fulfilled, a

---

2. On the historical and theological background of Christian weddings, see James E. White, *Introduction to Christian Worship* (Nashville: Abingdon, 2000), 276–86; and Michael Fowler, "Marriage," in ed. Robert E. Webber, *The Complete Library of Christian Worship, Vol. VI: The Sacred Actions of Christian Worship* (Peabody, MA: Hendrickson, 1993), 273–86.

couple was considered married regardless of the role the church played in a wedding ceremony.

This tentative relationship between secular marriage and religious blessing of the wedding, however, gave way to a singular partnership of the two as marriage came to be understood as one of the seven sacraments of the church. Marriage almost did not make the list of sacraments; but once it did later in the Middle Ages, the church took more direct control of the wedding ceremony and began adding theological language to it, describing what made a marriage. Especially added to requirements of consent, consummation, and cohabitation was the declaration of the marriage by the priest: "I now pronounce you husband and wife." In other words, whereas before the couple made the marriage with the church witnessing, now the church married the couple.

The Protestant Reformers rejected the idea of marriage as a sacrament, but continued the practice of performing weddings so that it clearly still had a sacrament-like standing as a church-moderated rite of passage. Thomas Cranmer, in his 1549 *Booke of Common Prayer*, developed a wedding service, "The Forme of Solemnizacion of Matrimonie," that drew together the theological understandings of marriage in his day with ritual language, and that has been influential in English-speaking cultures ever since:

> Dearly beloved friends, we are gathered together in the sight of God, and in the face of his congregation, to join together this man and this woman in holy matrimony, which is an honorable estate instituted of God in paradise, in the time of man's innocency, signifying unto us the mystical union that is betwixt Christ and his Church: which holy estate, Christ adorned and beautified with his presence, and first miracle that he wrought in Cana of Galilee, and is commended of Saint Paul to be honorable among all men; and therefore is not to be enterprised, nor taken in hand inadvisedly, lightly, or wantonly, to satisfy men's carnal lusts and appetites, like brute beasts that have no understanding: but reverently, discreetly, advisedly, soberly, and in the fear of God. Duly considering the causes for which matrimony was ordained. One cause was the procreation of children, to be brought up in the fear and nurture of the Lord, and praise of God. Secondly it was ordained for a remedy against sin, and to avoid fornication, that such persons as be married, might live chastely in matrimony, and keep themselves undefiled members of Christ's body. Thirdly for the mutual society, help, and comfort, that the one ought to have of the other, both in prosperity and adversity. Into which holy estate these two

> persons present: come now to be joined. Therefore if any man can
> show just cause why they may not lawfully be joined together: Let
> him now speak, or else hereafter ever hold his peace. [3]

In Cranmer's ritual three primary theological purposes for marriage are declared: procreation, control of lust (sexual morality), and the mutual (economic, emotional, physical) benefit of the two joining together. We shall discuss each in turn.

We begin with procreation. In the twentieth century, Protestants basically removed procreation from the list of *essential* purposes of marriage (although most would have still argued that marriage was the appropriate locale for having children). There are numerous theological, ethical, and practical reasons for dropping procreation as an essential purpose of Protestant marriage, such as the changing role of women in society, the population explosion, a scientific understanding of fertilization issues/problems, and the development and widespread use of birth control—giving couples a choice whether or not to have children.

Dropping procreation from the list of theological purposes for marriage has meant that sexual morality and mutual blessing to the couple are the two theological rationales Protestants have really held on to in their theology of marriage. Both of these reasons for marriage are as appropriate for a gay couple as a straight one. Procreation is only brought back into the discussion of marriage these days by Protestants when they are arguing *against* gay marriage.

The second theological purpose of marriage in this tradition is sexual morality. The church has long held that sex outside of marriage—that is fornication or adultery—is sinful. The problem with this ethical stance for homosexuals is that since marriage has been denied them, any sexual activity is by definition sinful.

This view has been alleviated somewhat by the sexual revolution of the 1960s and '70s. Many people in American culture, including Christians and faithful members of the church, have come to recognize that not all sex outside of marriage is sinful. This ethical transition, however, should not mean "anything goes" in terms of sex. Sexual activity that breaks the boundaries of consent, mutuality, and *hesed* towards one's sexual partner is sinful. By this standard, sex between persons of the same gender can be moral outside of marriage. Still, the highest expression of fidelity in an

---

3. Full text of the wedding service can be found at http://justus.anglican.org/resources/bcp/1549/Marriage_1549.htm.

intimate relationship is marriage. Thus the institution of marriage should be offered to all couples, regardless of sexual orientation, so that all can strive for this highest expression of intimacy.

The third theological value of marriage named in the traditional wedding ceremony is that of mutual benefit. The joining of a couple establishes a permanent situation in which each partner consistently contributes to the well-being of the other. This is the very definition of *hesed*. Well-being, as Cranmer defines it, includes economic, emotional, and physical support. There is nothing about this value that is specific to heterosexual couples. Why in the world would a society or a religious community not want a loving, committed, gay couple to experience this kind of mutual well-being?

Given that procreation is no longer valued as a theological purpose for marriage, we see that sexual morality and mutual benefit are two values that should be lifted up for gay couples just as they are for straight couples. It is often claimed that gay marriage is a challenge to heterosexual marriage and destroys traditional family values. Actually, the opposite is true. Extending the right to marry to gay couples takes nothing away from straight couples and in fact *affirms* family values. Same-sex marriage does not affirm gender complementarity, but it does lift up the importance of sexual morality in and through marriage and the mutual benefit of the institution of marriage. Officiating and preaching at a union ceremony or wedding for a gay couple means establishing for homosexuals the stability of marriage that has always been valued by the church.

HOMILETICAL STRATEGIES

Longitudinal Strategies

In the next section dealing with sermon-specific strategies, we will address some things to consider when developing a homily for a same-sex union or wedding. Longitudinal homiletical strategies, however, take us outside of those ceremonies themselves. In other words, we need to consider preaching in two other contexts that give support to liturgy and preaching in gay marriage and blessings of unions.

The first such context is week-in and week-out Sunday morning sermons. Preachers should not wait until the moment they are officiating at a same-sex wedding to talk about the importance of the right to marriage or the meaning of a Christian marriage as extending to same-sex couples. By including the issue and interpretation of gay marriage in regular worship, we will establish a sense of the gospel offered to all in the gift of marriage that sets up naming that gift in relation to any particular couple we join in a wedding. In other words, we should raise the issue of gay marriage occasionally in our regular sermons so that those listening closely will recognize we are repeating ourselves when we preach at a same-sex wedding.

The second context outside of same-sex weddings and union ceremonies to be considered in terms of homiletical strategies helping us preach at those weddings and union ceremonies is heterosexual weddings. Recall the scenario that began Chapter 1. At an opposite-sex wedding, you are careful to use language that avoids a patriarchal construct of marriage. At the reception after the ceremony, however, a lesbian in attendance pointed out how the liturgical language you used assumed gender complementarity as the theological foundation for marriage, thus excluding her and her partner from ever having access to the institution of marriage. Defining marriage at a heterosexual wedding in terms of heterosexuality precludes any proclamation at a homosexual wedding that claims marriage is a gift from God offered to all.

While at a heterosexual wedding we want to relate the liturgy and homily specifically to the couple being joined together and want to pronounce them "wife" and "husband," we should only use theological (and cultural) language to describe the purposes and promises of marriage in general that we would also use at a gay wedding. By developing a common liturgy and some standard homiletical language to describe marriage (analogous to the use of standardized language in funeral homilies as suggested in the next chapter), over time we reinforce the idea that the gift of marriage belongs to all, regardless of sexual orientation.

Sermon-Specific Strategies.

Ironically, the traditional structure of the Christian wedding ritual continues to reflect the ancient and medieval secular practices in which the couple serve as the primary actors in the ceremony, not the minister officiating at the ceremony. The ceremony begins with a declaration of free and clear intent of the couple to marry and leads to their making of vows of fidelity and mutual benefit to one another. The minister witnesses, records, and blesses/pronounces the marriage to be fact as a response to their actions.

The minister, as one who acts on behalf of the church and of the state, is not superfluous to the ritual, but neither are her or his actions central to the wedding. That being the case, it can be stated explicitly that proclamation is an unessential part of the wedding ceremony. Many marriages have been formed at weddings without sermons. Yet while proclamation may not be required for a wedding to take place, it is an essential element of Christian worship. Thus, if the church is to offer a wedding to a couple as part of its worship offering to God (as opposed to being a wedding chapel), proclamation should be included.

The primary purpose of a wedding or union ceremony homily, whether the couple joining together is gay or straight, is to proclaim God's good news in light of the couple joining together and their intention to live together in light of that good news. It is not a time for moral exhortation or teaching on the doctrine of marriage. It is a celebration of God's gift of *hesed* as offered to the world through Jesus Christ and manifested in this particular moment of grace and the particular relationship being formed in this particular wedding. In other words, in the wedding homily, marriage is the occasion for the proclamation, not the whole of its content. The particular couple's decision to make a mutual, lifelong, public commitment to one another is the primary illustration of the sermon, if you will. As an illustration, it is not the focus of the sermon, but the lens through which to view the focus: God's good news for those gathered in worship.

Preaching to those gathered at a wedding or union ceremony is complicated by the fact that unlike the Sunday morning sermon, in the wedding homily the preacher addresses a two-tiered congregation. The primary audience for the homily is the couple. The preacher uses their joining together as the central illustration to proclaim to them God's love offered to, for, and through them. Those who have gathered to witness and celebrate the union are the secondary audience for the preacher. The words of the homily may be directly spoken to the couple with the witnesses placed in a mode of overhearing, but the preacher must always shape the content for the whole community.

There is a secondary purpose for the wedding homily that is unique to gay weddings or union ceremonies in contrast to heterosexual weddings. This is a political purpose. Clergy are servants of the state as well as of the church when performing straight weddings. We must be licensed and recognized by the county clerk, and sign the license by virtue of being authorized by the state. So performing a straight wedding has a political

function, but because of heteronormative structures in society, this political function need play no role in the sermon. Performing a gay wedding,
in a day when gay weddings are not legal everywhere, is a different sort
of political action. It is an act of social justice and thus a sermon at a gay
wedding must include calls for social justice. The sermon should include
an expression of the hope that God's *hesed* will be offered in the form of a
marriage to all who would want it, gay or straight.

Preachers must be careful not to allow this secondary purpose to become primary, however. As many straight couples want church weddings
for cultural reasons instead of religious ones, some gay couples may want
church weddings or union ceremonies out of cultural-political reasons and
not religious ones. The preacher as a representative of God and the church
helps the couple form a *Christian* marriage/union, and thus the religious
dimension must be primary in a way that includes the political dimension.

Preaching these two purposes cumulatively will help the community
of faith that sponsors these services and whom the pastor represents as-
similate the idea that gay and straight unions are theologically the same,
and thus feel compelled to work to transform the church and culture so
that gay couples can be treated equally in terms of access to legal marriage.

Sample Wedding Homily

CHOOSING A BIBLICAL TEXT for a same-sex wedding is difficult in that the heteronormativity of Scripture means there are no texts that directly affirm homosexual love or marriage. In the sermon below, this problem is named and a text (Song of Solomon) that lifts up heterosexual love in quite evocative ways is claimed as representative of the quest for intimate love in general—that is, regardless of sexual orientation. To help make this hermeneutical move even more effective, the passage that is chosen for the homily is a place in the text where the woman is speaking of her male lover (using male pronouns frequently). Little in the passage itself indicates a woman is speaking. Having this read before the homily by a male voice obscures the heterosexual nature of the relationship portrayed in the text and simply lifts up the quest for love. This allows the sermon to name the heterosexual context of the text exegetically while diminishing its importance homiletically.

This usurping of a heterosexual text to name the same intimate love found in a homosexual relationship as a gift from God parallels well to the political reality behind the homily. The couple has fought to be able to claim marriage (which has been reserved for opposite-sex couples) as their right, and have only just now been able to be legally married in their state. They are not claiming heterosexual love or marriage as theirs to have. They are claiming love and marriage affirmed for heterosexuals is something they already have, and they want it affirmed equally for them as well. The wedding is a celebration of that political reality coming to be.

One final word of introduction of a different sort is helpful to note. The sermon quotes Martin Luther as distinguishing between the intoxicating love of a new couple and the more mature "sincere love" of married life. The sermon affirms Luther's general sentiment but also pushes a little against the idea that intoxication must be lost for "sincere love" to arise. The reason that this is important to note is that this language is worked into all of the preacher's wedding homilies. Anyone who has attended opposite-sex weddings at which the preacher officiated for congregants would recognize that the same language is being applied to same-sex love and marriage. Distinctions between types of love or marriage are erased.

SONG OF SOLOMON 3:1–5

¹ *Upon my bed at night*
  I sought him whom my soul loves;
  I sought him, but found him not;
  I called him, but he gave no answer.
² *"I will rise now and go about the city,*
  in the streets and in the squares;
  I will seek him whom my soul loves."
  I sought him, but found him not.
³ *The sentinels found me,*
  as they went about in the city.
  "Have you seen him whom my soul loves?"
⁴ *Scarcely had I passed them,*
when I found him whom my soul loves.
I held him, and would not let him go
  until I brought him into my mother's house,
  and into the chamber of her that conceived me.
⁵ *I adjure you, O daughters of Jerusalem,*
  by the gazelles or the wild does:
  do not stir up or awaken love until it is ready!

HOMILY

You two look a little tired to me. You dressed up so nice and look so good that everyone else may have missed it, but you're sort of panting from running a good race. It's no wonder you're tired, of course. It takes so much to pull a wedding together.

- Finding a wedding date that will work for everybody.
- Reserving the church.
- Meeting with the minister for forced premarital counseling an ungodly number of times.
- Choosing between roses, tulips, or calla lilies. But you don't just get to choose the *type* of flower; no, you have consider, analyze, and argue about which *color* flower to have.

- Picking out the attire for the couple and for the attendants. Getting sized. Changing your minds about what to wear. Deciding how much you want to punish attendants for what they made you wear at their weddings.

- Ordering a specific type of cake after tasting forty cakes that all taste the same.

- Hiring a caterer for the reception; picking out the food and the champagne. And making sure your DJ is cool enough to avoid the chicken dance but might be willing to play the bunny hop—you know, just for the kids attending.

No wonder you're tired. I'm tired just listing off all these things you had to do to pull off a wedding over the last few months. And as if this list wasn't long enough, you two have to be overachievers and go and spend a couple of decades fighting for homosexual love to be accepted in society, fighting for same-sex weddings to be legalized in this state, and fighting to get the church to perform weddings for gay couples just like we have always done for straight couples. No wonder you're tired.

Ah, but what a good tired it is. Finally, the church has done what is right. Finally, the state did what is right. And, finally, this allowed you to do what you have known was right for you two for a long time: to get married.

But, of course, Alex and David, I know something about you two that perhaps not everyone here knows. I know you stand here today as big, fat liars. You pretend to come get married . . . when you're already married. Even though the church and the government didn't recognize it, you and some friends and family gathered on a mountaintop seven years ago today, and you two made vows to one another and declared yourselves married. And so you were in your own eyes, in the eyes of your friends and family, and in the eyes of God. So today we really come together to affirm your marriage as you take a step withheld from you seven years ago, to allow you to say in this house of God the promises you said seven years ago on the mountain of God, to let the eyes of the church and the government catch up with what you and God have seen for some time now.

We celebrate today that God has given you two a sustained and sustaining love for each other that grows out of God's eternal love for each of you. Martin Luther wrote all the way back in the sixteenth century,

> It is the highest grace of God when love continues to flourish in married life. The first love is ardent, is an intoxicating love, so that

we are blinded and are drawn to marriage. After we have slept off
our intoxication, sincere love remains in the married life of the
godly . . .

Well, seven years later and your desire to marry—remarry—in this way is
clearly a sign of God's gift of sincere love.

Still, far be it from me to disagree with the great Martin Luther, but I
would hope that sincere love does not *completely* displace love that intoxi-
cates. I assume the romantic gesture of you two having this second wedding
testifies to the fact that in marriage intoxication may evolve, may mellow,
but need not ever disappear. Indeed, it would seem that sincere marital love
by its very definition must include a spark of intoxication.

The Song of Solomon is one of the most puzzling books of the Bible.
It is a beautiful collection of love poems in which a male lover and a female
lover are in dialogue. They are intoxicated with one another. What is puzzling about the book is the fact that God is never once mentioned in it. Why
in the world is a book that doesn't mention God included in the Bible?

Listen again to part of the poem from chapter 3 that was read just
before the sermon. The woman is speaking:

Upon my bed at night
        I sought him whom my soul loves . . .
"I will rise now and go about the city . . .
        I will seek him whom my soul loves."
I sought him, but found him not.
The sentinels found me,
        as they went about in the city.
"Have you seen him whom my soul loves?"
Scarcely had I passed them,
        when I found him whom my soul loves.
I held him, and would not let him go . . .

The woman in this poem speaks of a longing not to be loved, but to love.
She isn't just looking for someone with whom she can be intoxicated. She is
looking for someone whom her very soul will love.

But she had been looking for love in all the wrong places. In her bed.
In town. In the nightlife. She asked others, even the police of all people, to
fix her up on a blind date. Then she just happened upon her love. Not someone for whom she had lust because he was handsome. Not someone who
entertained her with his wit and charm. Not someone who owned a large

farm and would provide her with all the comforts of life. No, she doesn't tell us anything about him, because at this point descriptions are useless. She doesn't love him because . . . she just loves him. She loves him with all of her emotional and physical being:

> When I found him whom my soul loves,
> I held him, and would not let him go.

Today you claim as your divine right a ceremony that has for most of history been reserved for heterosexuals. So I invite you to claim this poem of a heterosexual couple as your own as well. Because the reason I think it is included in the Bible has nothing to do with being straight. I think the reasons ancient Jews and Christians seated the Song of Songs right next to Genesis and Psalms and Isaiah and Matthew and Romans and Revelation at the scriptural dinner table was to say that romantic, intoxicating, and sincere love is a gift from God to the *whole* of humanity right alongside the gifts of creation, liberation, forgiveness, comfort, and hope. I believe at the core of my being that this kind of love is a gift from God to you, David, through Alex and to you, Alex, through David. And having witnessed the reception and regifting of that divine gift of love between the two of you all these years, it is my honor—it is *our* honor—to now serve as witnesses as you remake your vows to each other, as you remarry each other for the very first time. And I pray that in your sincere and intoxicating married love, you finally get the rest you so deserve.

5

Funerals and Memorial Services

THE PHONE RINGS AT 1:30 in the morning. That always means one of two things for a pastor: an emergency call to the hospital or rushing to someone's home following a death. In this case, the two are combined. Dewayne has taken his own life.

When you arrive at the hospital, a social worker takes you to a room where the family is gathered, crying violently, and asking why Dewayne would do this. You know elements of the answer but cannot share them because you promised Dewayne that you would hold his sexual orientation in confidence. He could not bear the thought of family rejection if his mother and siblings found out, but struggled with leading two separate lives. You offer a prayer, make some arrangements to meet at the funeral home tomorrow, and remain just to be present with the family as long as they wish.

An hour later you leave the room and walk to your car. There Jon is leaning against the hood waiting on you. Jon is (now, was) Dewayne's boyfriend. The family knew nothing of him, and he would not be able to enter their inner circle of mourners. He would make no decisions concerning the funeral arrangements. He could not even go into the hospital to say goodbye to Dewayne. You spend time with Jon, offer a prayer, and make arrangements to connect with him at his apartment tomorrow.

Driving home you are overwhelmed with the tension of naming Dewayne, naming God's love for Dewayne, and making some slender piece of sense of Dewayne's suicide for two different groups at the funeral—those who did not know Dewayne was gay and those who did. How do you honor the different identities Dewayne chose to share with the two groups while keeping his secret from some? How do you avoid outing him after his death without dishonoring the relationship he had with Jon? What in the world will you say when you stand to preach the gospel in light of this young man's death?

PURPOSES OF FUNERALS AND MEMORIAL SERVICES

Funerals and memorial services have three primary purposes.[1] The first is to care for the deceased, specifically to commit the remains to their resting place and commend the life or soul of the deceased into God's care. This has always been the primary purpose of funerals, whether Christian or otherwise. In our therapeutic age, however, the church has focused on the grieving and left the care of the deceased to the funeral directors (with the result that it is often an economic hardship on the family). Funeral directors prepare the body for viewing and burial or cremation. Without concerning ourselves with these specific roles, pastors need to reclaim the care for the deceased in our ministry.

Whether we are officiating at a funeral (at which the body is present) or a memorial service (at which the body is not present, but cremains may or may not be), pastors are to be concerned with the physical reality of the deceased's life and death. We do this in a number of ways. We need to name death explicitly and not euphemistically—we may claim that Christ has conquered death, but death in all its pain, tragedy, and finality is a reality. We lead the casket from the church or funeral home and from the hearse to the grave. And whether burying, interring, or scattering remains, we speak ancient words of ashes to ashes, dust to dust. But all of these actions relate to having named the deceased as an embodied person instead of (as is too often done) focusing only on a soul that has now escaped the body and flown off to heaven. God created the person as a fully human, fully embodied being, and we must honor that reality in the funeral or memorial service. Applied to the issue of overcoming heterosexism that concerns us in this book, caring for the embodied deceased when the person was gay means that in addition to offering traditional liturgical formulas over the casket at the graveside, we must appropriately but more explicitly include

1. These three purposes are defined in conversation with Paul P. J. Sheppy, *Death Liturgy and Ritual: Volume I: A Pastoral and Liturgical Theology* (Burlington, VT: Ashgate, 2003); and Thomas G. Long, *Accompany Them with Singing: The Christian Funeral* (Louisville: Westminster John Knox, 2009).

in the naming of the person's physical existence the sexual orientation and intimate relationships that filled the person's life and surround her or him in death.

Commending the deceased into God's care, likewise, implies naming the person with integrity and respect. As we would not offer Frank up to God while calling him Tom, we should not commend a homosexual into God's care using heteronormative language or assumptions in naming his or her life and relationships. For example, we would never avoid naming a loving, intimate heterosexual relationship in a funeral sermon. To simply not name homosexual partners leaves the impression in a heterosexist world that the deceased was heterosexual.

That said, the pastor must be careful not to out the deceased when they had not chosen to come out of the closet on their own. Whether in relation to family, church, employment, or the wider society, they may have been avoiding rejection and hardship by keeping their sexual identity hidden from some people and institutions. We should not add to their oppression after the fact in the name of being prophetic by making epiphanies they did not choose to make while alive and which they cannot interpret now that they are dead.

The second purpose of funerals and memorial services is to comfort the bereaved. We preachers are well aware that those who gather for a funeral experience grief in very different ways. Some wail openly while others show no facial expressions. Some focus only on the deceased and others reflect on their own mortality. As pastors, though, we move ahead and assume that God will comfort them all and all of them can and will (hopefully) take from the liturgy, eulogy, and sermon what they need.

Add to this dynamic, however, the fact that those who gather represent a wide spectrum of relationships with the deceased, and the challenge for the preacher increases. How do we offer a word in our sermon that names the deceased and God's care for her or him in a way that parent, spouse, child, friend, coworker, and acquaintance all receive the level of comfort they need? Preachers usually concern themselves with comforting those who are closest to the deceased because they are the ones in the most pain. If we are able to offer them a bit of comfort, then surely the others who experience this person's death in a more distant manner will be comforted as well. This applies to preaching at the funeral of a gay person just as it does to a straight person—that is, if the gay person is out of the closet.

If the attitudes of others and the circumstances of the deceased's life, however, had forced her or him to remain in the closet with some, preachers may find themselves in a different bind than comforting those with different levels of grief. We may have to deal with two communities at the same time—heteronormative/heterosexist family and friends on the one hand and partners and gay and allied friends on the other. Both communities are likely to experience grief at very deep levels, but they have no connection with each other. The first group may not even have knowledge of the other and not recognize them at the funeral. Likely, the two groups know the deceased almost as if he or she were two different people, living two different lives, holding two different sets of values.

Or to complicate matters further, perhaps the deceased was openly gay but some of those who gather for the funeral because they cared for the deceased and feel the pain of her or his death deeply nevertheless consider homosexuality wrong. They may have rejected the person outright (and yet still be in charge of funeral arrangements!) or stayed in some form of tense relationship with the person (ranging anywhere from forcing the person as a minor into reparative therapy to keeping their mouth shut but praying that she or he not end up in hell).

In these types of scenarios, the preacher must find ways to address the different groups in attendance in different ways at the same time if all are to be offered the comforting grace of the gospel. We will discuss this in more depth below under "Homiletical Strategies," but we should assert clearly here the theological and liturgical mandate that we cannot simply choose to address one group of mourners over against another. The gospel we preach has been offered to all, therefore we must find ways to speak it to all.

This leads us to the third purpose of funerals and memorial services. In addition to caring for the deceased and comforting the bereaved, funerals proclaim God's resurrecting power, love, hope, and life in the face of a particular death. The first two purposes are, of course, accomplished when this third one is done well. The deceased is best cared for and compassion for those filled with grief is best offered when the good news of Jesus Christ is presented with authenticity and power. For the gospel to be proclaimed effectively in this manner, preachers must be absolutely clear and explicit in their funeral sermons for homosexuals that God's salvific love is given to homosexuals freely just as it is to all. There can be no room for confusion among the hearers in which they think we assert that God condemns the deceased because of his or her sexual orientation or that God loves the deceased in spite of his or her sexual orientation.

THEOLOGY OF LIFE, DEATH, AND ETERNAL LIFE

The three purposes of funerals and memorial services—caring for the deceased, comforting the bereaved, and proclaiming the gospel in the face of a particular person's death—call on us to pause and comment on the content of theology that preachers bring to bear on them. Neither the focus nor the length of this book, however, allows us to offer a fully developed theology of the nature of human life, death, and life after death. Moreover, the river of eschatological perspectives running through the church is so deep and wide that we could hardly do justice to any of the currents given our focus. Some Christians see the essence of human existence as a soul that separates from the body at death, while others reject such dualism and argue that human existence is by definition embodied existence. Some Christians say there are states of individual existence after death signified in concepts of heaven, purgatory, hell, or resurrection of the body; others claim a corporate vision of being incorporated into God's eternal being; and still other Christians claim that language of the afterlife is metaphorical for pre-death existence participating in God's eternal life and when we die we die.[2] Fortunately, the question before us is much narrower: what theology of human existence, death, and eternal life do preachers need to share when the particular death being addressed is that of a homosexual as opposed to a heterosexual?

The obvious answer to this question is that the theology we affirm in liturgy and in our sermon at the funeral of a gay person should be exactly the same as that which we offer at a funeral of a straight person. We assume a common humanity—death does not affect some people in one way and another group of people in a different way. Moreover, we assume that in Christ there is no longer Jew or Greek, slave or free, male or female;

2. For a review of the various stances concerning death and life after death see Terence Nichols, *Death and Afterlife: A Theological Introduction* (Grand Rapids: Brazos, 2010). For a historical survey of the development of views of the afterlife see Alana F. Segal, *Life after Death: A History of Afterlife in Western Religion* (New York: Doubleday, 2004). Finally, for an overview of other religious views of the afterlife (many of which are uncritically assimilated into popular Christian thought), see ed. Harold Coward, *Life after Death in World Religions* (Maryknoll, NY: Orbis, 1997) and ed. Jacob Neusner, *Death and the Afterlife* (Cleveland: Pilgrim, 2000).

gay or straight (see Gal 3:28). As in our baptism we are all one in Christ, we who die in Christ all die the same death—a death that does not have ultimate power over us. Thus whatever we affirm that follows death, we affirm it for all Christians, not just straight Christians. God's *hesed* does not discriminate. Our theology of life, death, and life eternal, then, is in no way modified by who we are burying.

To affirm this stance, preachers need to make sure to be consistent in the presentation of these theological categories from one funeral to the next so that congregants who attend services for different sisters and brothers in Christ recognize that we view the gay person's life, dying, and death as held by God in exactly the same way God holds all people at the end of human existence. Indeed, when we not only present a consistent theology but repeatedly use the same language to present that theology in the funerals of both heterosexual and homosexual people we bury, we implicitly offer the message that God companions all of us throughout our lifespan as well as into and beyond our dying and death.

For example, some homiletical language that can be used in funerals and memorial services to express a clear confidence in God's providential and salvific care in the face of death without requiring those in the gathered assembly to all believe the same thing about eternal life involves reading Romans 8:31–39 and saying something like,

> When someone dies people often say, "Well, it was her time and she's with God now." They mean well. They are trying to make sense of death or are trying to offer comfort. But to say someone is with God after death distorts the good news of the gospel. The good news of Jesus Christ who showed us that nothing can separate us from God's love, nothing in life and not even death, is that God is with Alice now just as God has *always* been with Alice. Alice's death has changed our situation. It has not changed God's.

The primary purpose for this sort of language is twofold: 1) to combat the idea that God picks the time of our deaths and takes loved ones away from us; and 2) to remind those gathered that the providential and salvific care of God does not start at death but has been a part of the deceased's life (and of our lives) all along. Using this language during the funeral for a gay person after having used it in funerals for straight people reminds all gathered that God in God's *hesed* was present in the life of the homosexual just as God is claimed to be present in the lives of heterosexuals. Presenting a consistently held theology concerning life, death, and eternal life in every funeral at which we officiate is a subtle but strong message that God in God's *hesed* accepted the person as homosexual, both in life and death.

In spite of the assertion that one's theology and the language to express that theology should be consistent between funerals for gay and straight people, there is reason to give certain theological affirmations a stronger, more explicit emphasis at a homosexual's funeral. Given widespread heteronormativity, heterosexism, and even homophobia, explicitly naming that the deceased was and is valued by God *as* a homosexual may be essential for some gathered, especially homosexuals who are there grieving and fearing how the church might respond to this death given its checkered past, to be able to hear and embrace the gospel. One way this can be done is to affirm explicitly that the deceased, like every human, was created in God's image, was created good, very good in line with the theology named in Chapter 1. To name this goodness in relation to the whole of human nature—the spiritual, emotional, and *physical* self—affirms that the embodied, sexual self is marked with God's *hesed*. Any hint that homosexuality is a perversion of original creation is squashed by the celebration of the deceased's life and love. Failing to preach the goodness of the created nature, on the other hand, can be understood by individuals in the gathered community as tacitly reinforcing the shame that often surrounds the death of a gay person simply because she or he was gay.

In addition to the possibility of emphasizing the theme of the deceased's created goodness, it can be important at times to emphasize the cross in relation to the death of a gay person before moving too quickly to the good news of the resurrection. Interpretations of the crucifixion can be offered from many different legitimate perspectives. At a funeral it is certainly appropriate to name that Christ died once *for all*, including for the deceased, so that she or he might "be united with him in a resurrection like his" (Romans 6:3–11).

This language of the universality of the salvific effects of Christ's death can serve as standard language (like that presented above) offered in the funerals and memorial services of both heterosexual and homosexual individuals. But as in the case of any tragic death, when a gay person dies as a result of AIDS, suicide, or violence, preachers should also claim explicitly that in the incarnate and crucified Christ, God has been a companion with the deceased in her or his dying and death. Such affirmation is especially important given that such forms of death of gay persons are not only tragic but often carry shame with them. AIDS has often been called the judgment of God and/or nature against homosexuality, instead of the ghastly, indiscriminate disease it is. Gay men and lesbians have been described as getting what they deserve when they are victims of deadly violence instead of being recognized as martyrs of sinful hatred. Moreover, the suicide of a gay person is rationalized by heterosexists in terms of the person not being able to live with her or his "unnatural" ways instead of recognized as being related to social pressures to be straight (i.e., "normal") and/or persecution for refusing to pretend to be straight.

Indeed, in the face of such terrible forms of death of a gay person, our care for the deceased, the difficulty of offering comfort to the bereaved, and the call to proclaim the gospel of the crucified Christ may require preachers not only to name that the manner of death is not a sign of sinfulness on the part of the deceased but also to take the next step and name the structural sin that contributed to his or her suffering and death. The tragic passion of Christ reveals that God has embraced the deceased in her or his tragic suffering, dying, and death, and lays bare the systemic sin that stigmatized the person on the basis of her or his sexual orientation leading in part or in whole to that individual's death. To say that Christ takes on our death (and the death of the deceased) can be interpreted as Christ's bearing the marks (stigmata) of violence and despair, and ultimately conquering them. This reminds those gathered that no matter how the deceased dies she was companioned by God throughout her lifespan and into her suffering and death.

HOMILETICAL STRATEGIES

Longitudinal Strategies

Eulogies and funeral sermons are not the same thing. A sermon or homily is a proclamation of the good news of Jesus Christ, while a eulogy is a remembrance of the deceased. Often in Protestant funerals and memorial services, however, the eulogy and the sermon are combined into a single monologue. The problem with this combination is that reminiscing about the deceased too often overshadows proclamation of the gospel.

One way for us to think of the funeral sermon containing the eulogy is that we are to proclaim the unconditional love (*hesed*) of God-in-Christ for all—love that is not even limited by death—using the deceased's life and death as our sermon imagery. This configuration, proclamation supported by eulogy, creates the proper hierarchy of functions while making both essential to the funeral. First, let us deal with the message of the gospel; then we will turn to the person's life and death as imagery that gives that message the specificity needed in the face of loss.

Too often in our therapeutic culture with our emphasis on the pastor as caregiver rather than priest, prophet, theologian, scriptural interpreter, and/or representative of the church, we unconsciously act as if the purpose of the funeral sermon is to make people "feel better" in psychological terms. A funeral, however, cannot do what is only possible with time. Grieving can continue for months and years. Thus, at the beginning of this process of mourning, the sermon is to ground the congregation, and especially the loved ones, in Christian hope (as discussed above).

Funeral sermons often have to be developed quickly. But we should remember that in some sense the sermonic claim for every funeral sermon we preach will be pretty much the same. How we develop that claim for each sermon will vary. But once we find some nuggets of homiletical language we find especially appropriate for naming Christian hope in the face of death (like the examples discussed above), we should use them as part of almost every funeral sermon we preach. This will save us time, but more importantly it will serve as significant teaching for our church members who hear us preach multiple funerals. If we have stock language that we use as part of most funeral sermons and use that language for the funerals of both heterosexual and homosexual people we bury, we implicitly offer the message that God loves and treats us all the same.

Let's turn from the general message of the gospel proclaimed to using the specific person's life and death as the imagery for sharing that message. All persons we bury are a mixture of saint and sinner, and it is important to remember that balance in naming the deceased in a funeral sermon. If we present the deceased as only a saint (with the idea that this will offer mourners comfort), those whom the deceased may have injured will be injured again by the sermon. On the other hand, it is not the preacher's place to offer judgment over the deceased, providing some kind of bulleted list of her or his sins (as if we could know them all). We proclaim the forgiving, resurrecting love of God-in-Christ in light of the complexities of individual humans and of the universal human condition.

In relation to our specific focus, as we named in relation to preaching on the human condition in Chapter 1, a deceased person's sexual orientation should not be the basis for naming the person as either sinner or saint. We absolutely want to avoid any language that names the deceased as in need of God's grace (which is a need we all have) in a way that hearers could interpret as us implying that the person's homosexuality is what needed divine forgiveness. Similarly, just because the person was gay and (likely) experienced hardships and oppression in relation to that identity did not make that person saintly.

That said, if the person was out of the closet, we should make sure to include elements of his or her life as a gay person when we use his or her life as imagery to carry the proclamation of Christian hope. This is important because in a heteronormative society, gay persons are either expected to be invisible or are seen and treated as "others" throughout most of their lives— that is, they are treated not simply as "different," but as "alien." To refrain from naming the person's sexual identity in the sermon is to create a disconnect between the gospel and the realities of being perceived as "other." Christian hope must contain within it the specific hope that the oppression that keeps some people as "others" will be overcome. Thus, we should not closet anyone at the end of their lives who chose to live as an out gay person in a heterosexist society. In this sense, then, as with wedding and unions, there is a religiopolitical element to the funeral of any gay person.

Having asserted that we need to be careful not to re-closet a gay person at whose funeral we are officiating, we should be careful in naming the person's sexual identity never to reduce a gay person to her or his sexual orientation. Even with the best of intentions such stereotyping fails to name the wholeness of the deceased's reality. We must consider the individual's education, family, career, relationships, world view, hobbies, interests, passions, and so forth if we are going to proclaim that God loved the person's whole heart, soul, strength, and mind.

Moreover, a special caveat should be added for straight pastors officiating at the funeral of a lesbian or gay man. Straight pastors must be careful not only to avoid stereotypes but also from unintentionally tokenizing a gay person who has died. Tokenizing can occur by using language to describe and telling stories about the deceased that serves to emphasize and give credibility our role as an ally. Overexposing and overemphasizing elements of the deceased's life related to her or his sexual orientation may be more about showing our comfort level with the person's sexual orientation than naming the person in a way that cares for the deceased and offers comfort to all those gathered.

Sermon-Specific Strategies

Turning from broad strategies related to proclaiming Christian hope at funerals and memorial services in relation to the death of a gay person, we focus now on strategies related to some specific circumstances that can arise when burying a homosexual in our society as opposed to circumstances that surround the burial of a heterosexual.

First, we have mentioned above the problem of preaching a funeral sermon when the deceased is closeted to some or all of those gathered. The preacher must respect the person's decision and be careful not to out him or her after death. On the other hand, the preacher must offer a word of God's *hesed* to those who knew the deceased as gay, especially if there was someone in an intimate relationship with the deceased.

What is called for then is the use of language with double meaning. Minority, oppressed groups have often used code language that would have a surface-level meaning to outsiders but a deeper significance to insiders. Christians, for instance, used the symbol of the fish to identify themselves to other Christians without giving themselves away to persecutors. African American slaves sang spirituals that retold biblical stories at the surface level and expressed hopes about the underground railroad on a deeper level. Different gay subcultures have developed different sorts of codes to be able to meet other gay people, determine where it is safe to congregate, and simply to be able to speak about their lives in public without being victimized.

A gay preacher may be in a position to use insider language that a straight preacher is not. A preacher who is an ally and to whom the deceased was out (or who knows of the deceased's sexual orientation without the person being explicitly out to her or him) should not try to speak like an insider in using language that has double meaning. Rather, straight preachers must find code language specific to the individual being buried. It is standard pastoral care practice to visit with loved ones before a funeral to gain insight, language, and images from the life of the deceased to use in the sermon/eulogy. If the deceased is a closeted homosexual and the pastor is able to offer pastoral care to a partner and/or gay and allied friends of the person separately from the family, then some of this insight, language, and imagery can come from those who knew the deceased as gay. Mentioning a partner or friends by name without specifying the nature of their relationship, while imperfect, can at least be a way to include them in remembering the deceased. Indeed, the preacher can even discuss with these people in advance ways that she or he will reference elements of the person's life as a homosexual that will invite them to hear with ears others will not share.

A second scenario that will require the preacher to speak in ways different from the average funeral homily is if the deceased was out but rejected by some (family or church members) in attendance at the funeral or memorial service. In this case the role of the preacher is more straightforward. Part of caring for the deceased and being true to the gospel requires the preacher to stand in solidarity with the deceased, affirming God's *hesed* as extended to homosexuals as much as to anyone else, and to this individual particularly. While a funeral is not an appropriate setting for unpacking in detail the kind of anthropology and soteriology we describe in Chapter 1 or addressing complex civil rights issues as discussed in Chapter 3, the preacher must present a picture of God's salvific care at the funeral that is consistent with the proclamation of salvation preached at other times. The message of salvation should be preached explicitly and unflinchingly as God's desire for the deceased.

That said, it is not the preacher's task to call out, guilt, or shame those at the gathering who have different views of homosexuality and/or the deceased particularly. We are to be prophetic, but, especially at a funeral, we must also be pastoral. The gospel that is to comfort, we offer to all. Thus naming God's *hesed* extended to the deceased as a lesbian or gay man must at the same time be an invitation for those who have rejected her or him on the basis of sexual orientation to experience God's grace and forgiveness and to view the deceased and other homosexuals anew, that is, as beloved children of God. We leave the response to them, but we make the invitation implicitly simply by claiming that God's love for the deceased included loving her or him *as* a homosexual, not in spite of her or his homosexuality.

A third circumstance that calls for special care by the preacher is if the funeral or memorial service is for a gay man who died due to complications related to having HIV/AIDS. More than 1.1 million people in the United States are living with HIV infection, and men who have sex with other men, especially young African American men, are most often affected by the virus. There are about 50,000 new HIV infections each year, with over 15,000 people with AIDS dying each year.[3] While education about and research into the prevention and care of HIV/AIDS has significantly advanced since

3. These statistics can be found on the website for the Centers for Disease Control and Prevention, http://www.cdc.gov/hiv/statistics/basics/ataglance.html. See also www.aids.gov.

the outbreak of the epidemic in the early 1980s, there is still a significant amount of stigma related to having HIV/AIDS and dying because of it. The church has been especially egregious in promoting this stigma with segments of the church claiming that the virus is God's judgment on homosexuals. While moderate and progressive congregations and denominations no longer use that language, the heritage of such speech along with the fact that some conservative corners of the church still speak in this fashion means that the stigma is alive and well.

Preachers must explicitly address this theological fallacy at the funeral of one who has died of complications related to HIV/AIDS. To remain silent is to allow those who want to hold on to a judgmental view of homosexuals to assume we hold such a view as well. We must make room for authentic lament to occur in the face of a terrible, untimely death while also affirming that the immanent God suffered with the diseased person in her or his suffering—just as we would affirm in a sermon at the funeral of someone who died from a heart attack, cancer, or an automobile accident. God does not act like a puppeteer taking the lives of individuals here and there as acts of judgment. To explicitly claim that a person being infected with HIV/AIDS is *not* a divine act is both to take a political stance and to defend the character of God.

A fourth and final circumstance that calls on the preacher to speak in new ways at a funeral is when the deceased committed suicide related to the ostracism and oppression experienced due to being gay. Preaching at a funeral of a suicide victim is always hard. Preaching in the wake of a suicide and also dealing with the dynamics of heterosexism and homophobia as an element leading to that suicide is all the more difficult.

Yet a pastor who serves LGBT members will likely encounter this scenario since it is estimated that approximately 30 percent of youth suicides are committed by homosexual youth. Stated from another angle, different studies estimate that perhaps three times as many LGBT youth have reported considering suicide than non-LGBT youth.[4] The stigma, discrimination, and bullying directed at homosexual youth can be unbearable to one who is too young and lacks significant support systems to deal with being "othered" in such dramatic ways during such a stressful developmental stage of life.

---

4. For a thorough discussion of this and related issues, see "Suicide Risk and Prevention for Lesbian, Gay, Bisexual and Transgender Youth," published by the Suicide Prevention Resource Center, http://www.sprc.org/sites/sprc.org/files/library/SPRC_LGBT_Youth.pdf.

As at any funeral of a suicide victim, it is important that preachers name the deceased as just that: a victim. To allow anyone to assume we consider suicide a sin is to victimize the deceased (and his or her loved ones) again. Depression and hopelessness are as much diseases as leukemia or meningitis. When depression and hopelessness has been caused not by a neurological chemical imbalance but by ubiquitous pain inflicted by a heterosexist society on a homosexual individual, it is an even sadder occasion.

Explicitly speaking out against heterosexism and homophobia at the funeral of a homosexual who committed suicide is a sociopolitical act, but it also fulfills the three purposes of a funeral. By naming the person as a victim, we care for his or her soul in the sense that we claim the God-given dignity of the person never given to them by sinful societal behaviors. We also offer comfort for the bereaved because they can view the death not as a sinful act but as sinfully caused. And, finally, we proclaim God's resurrecting power, love, and hope in the face of this particular death by naming God as suffering with the person in life and making absolutely clear that even a death at one's own hands cannot separate us from the love of God.

Sample Funeral Homily

THE FOLLOWING HOMILY WAS delivered at the funeral of a seminary student—we will call her Marcia—who died of a genetic disease not long after graduation and ordination. She had struggled with the condition since early childhood and had to endure hospitalization and dangerous surgeries several times during seminary. There was much to deal with pastorally in naming Marcia before God.

But the situation to be named in the funeral sermon was more complicated due to the fact that while at seminary Marcia entered into a relationship with another woman, with most of her seminary colleagues and close friends outside of seminary knowing she was lesbian. Most of her family, however, was unaware of both her sexual orientation and her committed relationship. Indeed, some were self-described fundamentalists who would have rejected and condemned her had they known. So the congregation at the funeral consisted of people to whom Marcia had revealed herself in different ways and whom, at least in part, would have a message addressed to them in different ways.

Marcia's partner, whom we'll call Abigail, had not been a part of decision making at the end of Marcia's life. In fact, when Marcia was taken off of life support surrounded by family, Abigail was out in the waiting room with other seminary friends. Abigail struggled between wanting her relationship with Marcia acknowledged in the funeral and with not wanting to out Marcia or herself to Marcia's family. With the preacher, she decided that it would be appropriate to mention her as Marcia's roommate, and she and her friends would know that that label carried more weight than sharing space and rent. To press further in a way that Marcia's family would not catch or be offended by, the sermon would mention the pets Marcia and Abigail owned together and talked about all the time. She would know that homiletical language describing the shared ownership of and care for pets would symbolize the level of commitment they had to each other and the hopes they had held for a life together.

The sermon also draws on the song "Seasons of Love," from the musical *Rent*, that Abigail described as Marcia's favorite song. Abigail also loved the musical because of the way it deals with homophobia. The explicit connection to Marcia that everyone would recognize was that Marcia used this song as her ringback tone on her cellphone. Implicitly, however, Abigail would know that 1) she suggested this song for the sermon and 2) its use was meant to condemn the heterosexism that forced Marcia to stay in the closet even at the point of death.

ROMANS 8:31–39

31 What then are we to say about these things? If God is for us, who is against us? 32 He who did not withhold his own Son, but gave him up for all of us, will he not with him also give us everything else? 33 Who will bring any charge against God's elect? It is God who justifies. 34 Who is to condemn? It is Christ Jesus, who died, yes, who was raised, who is at the right hand of God, who indeed intercedes for us. 35 Who will separate us from the love of Christ? Will hardship, or distress, or persecution, or famine, or nakedness, or peril, or sword? 36 As it is written, "For your sake we are being killed all day long; we are accounted as sheep to be slaughtered." 37 No, in all these things we are more than conquerors through him who loved us. 38 For I am convinced that neither death, nor life, nor angels, nor rulers, nor things present, nor things to come, nor powers, 39 nor height, nor depth, nor anything else in all creation, will be able to separate us from the love of God in Christ Jesus our Lord.

FUNERAL HOMILY

You know what saying I hate today? It's not a saying I ever really liked, but today I hate it. You know what it is? "The good die young." I don't hate it because it's a lie. I don't hate it because it's cliché. I don't hate it because it's used in bad songs. I hate it today because it hurts. I hate it today because Marcia was too good and too young to die.

Measure it. It was only a few years ago that she entered the world kicking and screaming. It was only a few months ago that she moved her clothes out of her drawers so that she had a place for her rock collection. It was only a few weeks ago that she served on the staff at church camp for the first time. It was only a few days ago that she entered seminary. It was only a few minutes ago that that she began fighting off aneurisms caused by her lifelong struggle with her genetic condition. And it was only a couple of seconds ago that she was ordained. Marcia was too good and too young to die.

Of course, length is only one way to measure a life. Maybe you know the song from the play *Rent*. It was written by Jonathan Larson, who died of complications due to Marfan syndrome the day of the play's first preview off Broadway. If you ever called Marcia you knew it because she used it as her ringtone and it played in your ear while you waited for her to answer. It's probably not the case, but I always suspected she intentionally waited until the last minute to answer, to make sure we had to hear as much of the song as possible. I think she meant it to be a little sermon to anyone who called her. A little statement of her philosophy of life:

> Five hundred twenty-five thousand six hundred minutes,
> Five hundred twenty-five thousand moments so dear,
> Five hundred twenty-five thousand six hundred minutes,
> How do you measure, measure a year?
>
> In daylight, sunsets, in midnights, in cups of coffee,
> In inches, in miles, in laughter, in striving,
> In five hundred twenty-five thousand six hundred minutes,
> How do you measure a year in the life?
>
> How about love?
> Measure in love.

What happens if we measure Marcia's life in love instead of minutes? Her death still saddens us, but maybe, just maybe, it doesn't seem quite as tragic. Marcia's life was too short but it was over-filled with meaningful relationships. Two sets of parents who couldn't have cherished her more and whom she couldn't have loved more. Friendships formed and kept throughout her life, stretching all the way from childhood through her schooling to her final moments in the hospital—we have heard memories offered by a few who loved her dearly. She and her roommate Abigail loved and were loved by two dogs that are as opposite as mania and depression. Mentors, guides, pastors, and teachers who saw her struggles with life as lessons we could learn from. Churches that nurtured her. If we speak in terms of the love Marcia gave and received in her personal relationships instead of duration of her days, the cup that was Marcia's life was overflowing onto the table from which all of us who knew her dine.

What happens if we measure Marcia's life in love instead of minutes? Marcia's life overflowed with ministry. You know, it was not only we gathered here who thought Marcia died too young. Marcia herself was angry and confused about that. But her emotions weren't some kind of self-pity, although that would have certainly been justified. Her emotions evolved around the question of the meaning of her life. Why would God call her into the ordained ministry only to let her die without having the chance to serve? I certainly understand her question, but I could see what you could see that Marcia couldn't see. I watched a young woman come to seminary and struggle through the fact that she initially felt inadequate for ministry because she was a woman and she was different. She had had few role models of women in ordained ministry and was scared to death to preach—only men stand in the pulpit. But once she stood there, once she spoke the gospel to the gathering of the faithful, and once she served in her field education setting, she recognized all the more that God had endowed her with the gifts for ministry. But then came the aneurisms. She had to leave seminary and head south for treatment. Afterward, she could have stayed home with family to care for her. It was safe there. In their love for her, that's what her parents wanted. But she was going to finish her MDiv and returned to school with support from friends like Abigail. And, by God and through Christ, she was going to be ordained; and it was a great day for all who gathered last summer and laid hands on her and said, "God claims you for ministry." What Marcia couldn't see that we can was that her graduating and her being ordained *was* her ministry to us—her persistence, her desire, her faithfulness to that calling is her continuing witness to the gospel of Jesus Christ.

Add to Marcia's righteous persistence, the fact that this woman who suffered for much of her life never allowed her faith to simply turn inward as a pie in the sky protection against the struggles of life. In class she would often be the one to join her voice to Job's when he questioned God for his suffering; she joined voices with Jesus who called out, "My God, my God, why have you forsaken me?"; she joined her voice to all of God's children who suffer. You might think a woman who was chronically ill would have as a favorite Scripture some story in which Jesus heals the sick or some Psalm of lament in which the oppressed prays for relief. But her favorite passage was the one we read earlier:

> God has told you, O mortal, what is good;
> and what does the Lord require of you

> but to do justice,
>
> and to love kindness,
>
> and to walk humbly with your God?

Even in her suffering, Marcia was concerned about the ethical, just treatment of all in the world. I understand her self-questioning about her ministry. But let's answer her now: how many of you were touched by Marcia's dedication to the church, by the way her faith informed her living, her suffering, and her dying? How many of you were inspired by her drive to master divinity and be ordained? How many of you have seen God in Marcia? [Raise hand.] If we speak in terms of Marcia's loving ministry instead of the amount of time she was ordained, the cup that was Marcia's life was overflowing onto the table from which all of us who knew her dine.

What happens if we measure Marcia's life in love instead of minutes? Marcia *throughout* her short life knew the eternal, unending, infinite love of God. Marcia experienced God's love through the guise of

> the two sets of parents who raised her,
>
> her extended family who supported her,
>
> the communities of faith in church and at camp
>
>> that formed her in the faith,
>
> the schools that challenged her to reach for new heights
>
>> in her understanding of God and the world,
>
> in friends and family who saw her through school and beyond,
>
> in the region of the Christian church that acknowledged
>
>> they saw in her someone called into the ministry.

God has always been with Marcia in many, varied ways. In our time of grieving, people are likely to offer family and friends words that are meant to be comforting but distort both the gospel of Jesus Christ and the character of Marcia's life. Words like, "Well, at least she's with God now." Marcia is not with God *now*. Marcia has *always* been with God, because God has *always* been with Marcia. The good news of Jesus Christ is that death has not changed that one iota. When those we care about die, we finite mortals are no longer able to give them our love because we have been separated from them. That's why our vows are "till death do us part." But Paul writes, "Neither death nor life . . . nor anything else in all creation will be able to separate us from the love of God in Christ Jesus our Lord." God is beyond the limits of mortality. There is nothing we can do and nothing that can happen to us that will make God stop loving us. In the midst of the feelings of confusion, guilt, anger, and sorrow that ache in our bones because Marcia died way too young, the good news about God that we need to cling to is that God loves her as much now in death as God always loved her in life. If we speak in terms of the divine love Marcia received and continues to receive from God instead of the number of her mortal days, the cup that is Marcia's life is overflowing onto the table from which all of us who know her dine.

There is much to be sad about today. But there is also reason to rejoice. In a word, we rejoice in resurrection. In the risen Christ, the timing and nature of Marcia's death is utterly powerless to define the meaning of her life. Marcia's life manifested love given and love received. Yes, we rejoice with a tear in our eye and a catch in our throat, but we rejoice. So let us sing the hymn Marcia herself chose for us to sing today: "Joyful, Joyful, We Adore Thee." When we measure Marcia's life in love instead of minutes, the only response is to offer God praise and thanksgiving.

Glossary

If pastors, both heterosexual *and homosexual, are to counter heterosex-*
ism in their sermons, they must be careful to properly use terminology related
to homosexuality and homosexual issues. They must avoid terminology that
is or can be understood to be derogatory or offensive while including language
and concepts in a supportive fashion. This glossary is not comprehensive but
is intended to cover the main technical and slang terms popularly in use these
days.

Some terms and symbols that were intended to be offensive or degrad-
ing to homosexuals, such as queer, queen, dyke, *and the symbol of the pink*
triangle have been reclaimed by the gay community and used within that
community in nonderogatory ways. However, preachers should be aware
that "insider speech," that is, language used by members of a marginalized
community, is not always appropriate for public discourse, especially when
appropriated by someone who is not gay or when used before an audience
that is not equipped to recognize the nuance of use. Where appropriate in the
entries below, we have offered advice concerning pulpit use of various terms.

While the main sections of the book focus on issues related to heterosex-
ism and homosexuality, the Glossary contains an array of terms related to
broader issues of sexual orientation and gender identity. The argument of the
book was focused in order to keep the topic manageable and to recognize that
the sociocultural and religious discrimination against different groups should
not be flattened to appear all the same. Public discourse surrounding issues of
sexual orientation and gender identity, however, are often combined or even
collapsed in a way that requires advocates to be familiar with the broader
range of terms and concepts.

(Note: Words in the definitions printed in small caps indicate other en-
tries in the Glossary.)

Advocacy – political action intended to educate the populace and influence public policy, in this case in relation to arguing for the CIVIL RIGHTS of LGBTQI individuals. Advocacy groups working on behalf of the GAY community are prevalent in North America and throughout the world as well as within most Christian denominations. Advocacy groups include Human Rights Campaign, GLAAD (Gay & Lesbian Alliance Against Defamation), and PFLAG (Parents and Friends of Lesbians and Gays).

Ally – generally, a person who is a member of the dominant group who works to end oppression in his or her own personal and professional life by supporting and ADVOCATING with the oppressed population. In this case, a HETEROSEXUAL individual, who works with the LGBTQI community in countering HETEROSEXISM and HOMOPHOBIA and all forms of prejudice and discrimination against sexual minorities.

Androgynous – lacking the physical characteristics (i.e., appearance and mannerisms) related to a specific GENDER identity; or conversely, having physical characteristics of both the masculine (from the Greek root *andr*, meaning "man") and feminine (*gynē* meaning "woman") genders, making it difficult to determine the gender of a person.

Asexual – a sexual ORIENTATION characterized by a lack of sexual attraction to either males or females. The prefix "a-" derives from the Greek meaning "not"; used in contrast to BISEXUAL, HETEROSEXUAL, and HOMOSEXUAL. Asexual should not to be confused with CELIBATE.

Behavior – theological and philosophical distinctions are sometimes made between HOMOSEXUAL actions and homosexual sexual ORIENTATION. At stake is the claim that while one's sexual orientation may not be sinful or wrong, his or her sexual behavior may be (thus the slogan, "Love the sinner, hate the sin"). This construct is a false dichotomy to be rejected in preaching. The distinction between behavior and orientation, however, is also used to indicate that sexual behavior does not necessarily dictate one's sexual orientation (e.g. a heterosexual person may experiment with homosexual behavior or a homosexual person may experimenting with heterosexual behavior).

Bicurious – usually used for heterosexual-identified men and women who experience some degree of SAME-SEX ATTRACTION. The prefix "bi-" derives from the Latin meaning "twice" or "double."

Bisexual – a sexual ORIENTATION characterized by sexual attraction to both males and females. The prefix "bi-" derives from the Latin meaning "twice" or "double"; in contrast to ASEXUAL, HETEROSEXUAL, HOMOSEXUAL.

Blessing – a religious ceremony recognizing the union of a gay couple. Such a ritual confers no legal standing for the couple, and thus stands in contrast to a wedding.

Butch – refers to lesbians or gay men who exhibit traditionally prescribed masculine qualities (physical attributes, clothing, and behavior), in contrast to those who are considered FEMME, drawing an analogy to stereotypical GENDER roles and attributes in HETEROSEXUAL relationships. While the term originated as a HETEROSEXIST insult and thus should never be used in the pulpit, *butch* has been reclaimed as acceptable slang within the GAY community by some.

Celibate – to abstain from sexual relationships (heterosexual, homosexual or bisexual). As opposed to ASEXUALITY, celibate people are sexually attracted to others but choose, often for religious reasons, not to engage in sexual contact.

Choice – (synonym for PREFERENCE; see LIFESTYLE) a HETERONORMATIVE term commonly used to support the argument that persons elect to be HOMOSEXUAL in contrast to arguments that sexual ORIENTATION is innate. The idea that people choose to be GAY is usually proffered by those who argue that homosexuality is unnatural because sexuality in nature is intended for reproduction. Thus homosexuals can and should choose to be HETEROSEXUAL if they wish. For those who argue that homosexuality is a sin, it must be a choice, since in this view people are heterosexual by nature (i.e., created as innately heterosexual). This term should be avoided in the pulpit, except in situations in which the concept is being disputed.

Civil Rights – legal, political and economic entitlements of individual citizens that are considered to be universal and protected by the government. When such rights are denied to minority groups, legal action, ADVOCACY, and even civil disobedience may be required to secure them. At stake in the debate concerning rights for HOMOSEXUALS is whether civil rights for the gay community are EQUAL RIGHTS or SPECIAL RIGHTS.

Civil Union – generally a legal contract available to HOMOSEXUAL couples in some states where SAME-SEX MARRIAGE is not a legal possibility. A civil union grants the couple a semblance of the legal and economic rights and benefits afforded to opposite-sex married couples (see DOMESTIC PARTNERSHIP). Many gay advocates and straight allies argue that civil unions are a step in the right direction of protection under the law but fall short of the full protections of marriage.

Closeted or "In the Closet" – a term for HOMOSEXUAL, BISEXUAL, and TRANSGENDER individuals who keep their sexual ORIENTATION, GENDER IDENTITY, behavior, and/or relationships hidden from family, friends, and/or the greater community. The term is at times extended to refer to a gay, lesbian, bisexual, or transgender person who has not admitted her/his sexual ORIENTATION to her/himself.

Coming Out – i.e., coming out of the CLOSET; when a HOMOSEXUAL, BISEXUAL, or TRANSGENDER individual reveals to others her or his sexual ORIENTATION or GENDER IDENTITY after it had been kept secret. The phrase can also refer to recognizing and naming oneself as homosexual, bisexual, or transgender. As opposed to a one-time event, "coming out" may be an ongoing and even lifelong process. October 11, the anniversary of the National March on Washington for Lesbian and Gay Rights in 1987, is celebrated as National Coming Out Day.

Conversion Therapy – synonym for REPARATIVE THERAPY.

Cross-dress – to wear clothes culturally associated with those stereotypically worn by persons of the opposite GENDER. See TRANSGENDER, DRAG QUEEN/KING, and TRANSVESTITE. Cross-dressing may be distinct from sexual attraction/ORIENTATION.

Domestic Partnership – generally a demographic or legal relationship in which a straight or gay couple cohabitates but is neither married nor joined by a CIVIL UNION (although in some states domestic partnership and civil union are synonyms). Domestic partners usually have fewer legal and economic rights and privileges than those who are married or in civil unions.

Drag Queen/King – a performer who CROSS-DRESSES and adopts the mannerism of an exaggerated stereotype of the opposite GENDER (see TRANSVESTITE). How *drag* came to be used for cross-dressing is debated. QUEEN refers to a male performer dressed as a woman and *king* to a female dressed as a man. Performing in drag may be distinct from sexual attraction/ORIENTATION. Because QUEEN is also used as a derogatory term for an effeminate homosexual male, this term should be avoided in the pulpit.

Dyke – a slur for a HOMOSEXUAL female. How the term came to be used in this way is unclear and debated. While the term originated as a HETEROSEXIST insult and thus should never be used in the pulpit, the term has been reclaimed as acceptable slang by some within the GAY community.

Equal Rights – legal, political ,and economic entitlements that apply uniformly to every person or citizen, regardless of race, sexual orientation, physical ability, political affiliation, religion, national origin, or age (see CIVIL RIGHTS). In the debate concerning rights for homosexuals, the term is primarily used in contrast to SPECIAL RIGHTS. For instance, is the right for a GAY couple to marry an equal right (all have the right to marry) or a special right (all have the right to marry a person of the opposite sex, not the right to marry someone of the same sex)?

Ex-gay – someone who once identified herself or himself as HOMOSEXUAL or BISEXUAL and claims to no longer to engage in homosexual behavior and/or be attracted to persons of the same sex. The term is related to the goal of REPARATIVE THERAPY of 'curing' GAY individuals through psychological and religious methods.

Faggot – often shortened to "fag," a slur for a HOMOSEXUAL male. How the term came to be used in this way is unclear and debated. While the term originated as a HETEROSEXIST insult and thus should never be used in the pulpit, the term has been reclaimed as acceptable slang by some within the GAY community.

Femme – refers to gay men or lesbians who exhibit traditionally prescribed feminine qualities (physical attributes, clothing, and behavior) in contrast to those who are considered BUTCH, drawing an analogy to stereotypical GENDER roles and attributes in HETEROSEXUAL relationships. While the term originated as a HETEROSEXIST insult and thus should never be used in the pulpit, the term has been reclaimed as acceptable slang by some within the GAY community.

Gay – slang synonym for HOMOSEXUAL. *Gay* can refer to both men and women or can be used for men in contrast to LESBIAN for women. In the 1920s, when *gay* was used by the general public to mean "happy," homosexuals used the word to indicate safe places frequented by homosexuals, as in a "gay club." The gay rights movement began to use the term publicly in the 1960s as an alternative to the more clinical-sounding term *homosexual*. *Gay* is also used inappropriately in a derogatory fashion to demean a person or action as inferior (e.g., "That's so gay"). While this latter use should never be heard in the pulpit, the former use is appropriate.

Gay Bashing – a form of HOMOPHOBIA that involves verbal and/or physical abuse by an individual or group of aggressors against another perceived to be homosexual. Gay bashing represents a spectrum running from verbal insults and slurs to bullying that involves violence (see HATE CRIME).

Gay Culture – drawn from the sociological/anthropological use of *culture* as a technical term, this label indicates that HOMOSEXUALS form within broader society a subculture characterized by shared experiences, values, language, and symbols. While this term (along with "gay community") is useful for the purposes of advocacy, it can inappropriately stereotype homosexuals as all sharing common values, lifestyles, aesthetics, activities, etc. It should be used in the pulpit only with great care to avoid any reductionist nuances.

Gay pride – the public affirmation of the self-worth and ADVOCACY for EQUAL RIGHTS of LGBTQI people.

Gay gene – refers to the ongoing scientific research to find a genetic origin for homosexuality. To date there is no unequivocal data to support or deny the theory that homosexuality is genetically determined. Some gay activists and ALLIES are wary of such a discovery because they are concerned that it might lead to forms of eugenics, while others place hope in such a discovery to aid the arguement that sexual ORIENTATION is innate instead of a personal CHOICE.

Gender – the socially constructed roles, behavior, activities, and attributes that a culture considers to be appropriately feminine or masculine. The term is contrasted with SEX as a technical biological/physiological term defining males and females.

Gender dysphoria – the diagnosis, identified in the *Diagnostic and Statistical Manual* of the American Psychiatric Association, for a person who feels and is distressed by a persistent incongruence between her/his experienced GENDER and assigned gender (see GENDER IDENTITY and TRANSSEXUAL).

Gender identity – individuals' subjective experience of their own gender. Originally the term was used in medical contexts to describe the need for SEX REASSIGNMENT SURGERY. Now, however, the term is applied more broadly to the spectrum of possible relationships in contrast to stereotypical gender roles.

Hate Crimes – bias-motivated violence, i.e. criminal violence targeting someone on the basis of their actual or perceived membership in a group despised by the aggressor(s). Targeted groups are characterized by race, ethnicity, national origin, religion, disabilities, class, sex, SEXUAL ORIENTATION, and GENDER IDENTITY. When laws are legislated concerning particular hate crimes, the result is increased penalties being imposed upon those found guilty of them. While federal hate crime laws related to racially motivated violence in the United States were instituted as part of the Civil Rights Act in 1968, it was not until after the murder of Matthew Shepard in 2009 that violence based on bias related to GENDER, GENDER IDENTITY, and sexual ORIENTATION (see

GAY BASHING) were added to the definition of a prosecutable hate crime. If a crime against a GAY person or group is not considered a federal offense, it can only be designated as a hate crime if the state has included sexual orientation in its list of targeted groups. (At the time of writing this book, only about half of the states do so.)

Hermaphrodite – in general biological terms, an organism that has reproductive organs associated with both male and female sexual functions; outdated application to humans who are born with both testicular and ovarian tissue (see instead INTERSEX). *Hermaphrodite* derives from Greek mythology, in which Hermaphroditus, the son of Hermes and Aphrodite, possessed the physical traits of both sexes. This term should be avoided in the pulpit.

Heteronormativity – the explicit or implicit and pervasive assumption by individuals and societies that HETEROSEXUALITY is the norm for biological SEX, GENDER IDENTITY, sexual ORIENTATION, and sexual relationships. This assumption grants heterosexuals a place of privilege in society and leads to the stigmatizing and harassment of LGBTQI persons as abnormal (see HETEROSEXISM).

Heterosexism – all forms of sexually prejudicial attitudes, actions, and structures rooted in HETERONORMATIVITY—e.g., denial of CIVIL RIGHTS, GAY BASHING, harassment, violence, and HATE CRIMES—that contribute to personal, institutional, and systemic discrimination of LGBTQI individuals and the LGBTQI community as a whole (compare HOMOPHOBIA).

Heterosexual – a sexual ORIENTATION characterized by sexual attraction to people of the opposite SEX. The prefix *hetero-* derives from the Greek meaning "different" or "other"; in contrast to ASEXUAL, BISEXUAL, HOMOSEXUAL. The terms *HETEROSEXUAL* and *HOMOSEXUAL* were coined together in the nineteenth century by a journalist attempting to differentiate in print between same-sex- and opposite-sex-attracted people.

HIV/AIDS – human immunodeficiency virus (HIV) compromises the body's ability to handle disease and can lead in its final stages of infectious development to acquired immune deficiency syndrome (AIDS), when one has severe difficulty fighting off disease and certain cancers. HIV is transmitted through bodily fluids, and thus is mainly spread by unprotected HETEROSEXUAL or HOMOSEXUAL sex and the sharing of apparatuses in illicit drug use. Thanks to advancements in medical research and care, being HIV positive is no longer a terminal diagnosis. Even though HIV/AIDS was never simply a "gay disease," culture has often depicted it in that manner in support of HETEROSEXISM.

Homophobia – literally "fear" (from the Greek root *phobos*) of homosexuals. The term was coined in 1968 to refer to heterosexual men's fear that others might think they are homosexual. It was quickly adopted by the gay community to refer to the prejudicial fear, hatred, and condemnation of LGBTQI persons. In this sense, homophobia and HETEROSEXISM are sometimes used as synonyms. In scholarly literature, however, *homophobia* is often used to refer to a narrower category of heterosexist expression that is found in fear-inspired and hateful bigotry toward GAYS (see the Introduction for a thorough discussion of this concept). *Internalized homophobia* – negative attitudes about one's own homosexuality, usually resulting from cultural heterosexist and homophobic messages. These negative attitudes about oneself can result in a range of thoughts, feelings, and behaviors, from shame and guilt to addictions and even suicide.

Homosexual – a sexual ORIENTATION characterized by sexual attraction to people of the same SEX. The prefix *homo-* derives from the Greek meaning "same"; in contrast to ASEXUAL, BISEXUAL, and HETEROSEXUAL. The terms *heterosexual* and *homosexual* were coined together in the nineteenth century by a journalist attempting to differentiate in print between same-sex- and opposite-sex-attracted people.

Inquiring – synonym for QUESTIONING.

Intersex – an umbrella term for congenital, hormonal, and/or chromosomal conditions in which a person is born with an ambiguous sexual/reproductive anatomy, i.e., having both male and female anatomical characteristics. The prefix *inter-* derives from the Latin meaning "between," indicating that an intersex person exists biologically on the spectrum between male and female sexes. Historically, doctors have encouraged parents of infants or children born intersex to rear them as *either* male or female, and to approve "corrective" surgery. Recently, however, people born intersex are advocating for the right to decide for themselves whether to identify as male, female, or intersex. Compare HERMAPHRODITE.

Lesbian – a female HOMOSEXUAL. Derives from the name of the Greek island, Lesbos, where the poet Sappho wrote, celebrating love between women in the sixth century BCE. The term came into use in medical literature of the late nineteenth and early twentieth century to describe female homosexual sexual behavior as a problem to be treated. The term is now accepted in popular and critical discussion and is appropriate for use in the pulpit.

LGBTQI – Acronym for LESBIAN, GAY, BISEXUAL, TRANSGENDER/TRANSEXUAL, QUESTIONING/QUEER, and INTERSEX/INQUIRING. The term is an umbrella for people who identify themselves as sexual minorities on the basis of sexual ORIENTATION and/or GENDER IDENTITY, and who thus find common interest in seeking public identity and CIVIL RIGHTS. The acronym is appropriate for use in the pulpit but will likely require explanation for some in the pews.

Lifestyle (i.e., gay lifestyle) – HETERONORMATIVE term referring to same-sex sexual behavior and identification within the GAY community or GAY CULTURE as a CHOICE rather than an expression of a person's innate sexual ORIENTATION. Use of the term is also a heterosexist approach to reducing the way all lesbians and gay men live to a stereotyped existence. The term should be avoided in the pulpit, except in situations in which the concept is being disputed.

Orientation (i.e., sexual orientation) – term commonly used to support the argument that persons are innately HETEROSEXUAL, HOMOSEXUAL, BISEXUAL, or ASEXUAL, in contrast to arguments that nonheterosexual sexualities are a CHOICE. The idea that nonheterosexual people have an innate sexual orientation is usually proffered by those in the GAY community and their ALLIES who argue that same-sex behavior is an expression of natural and healthy sexual attraction. Thus homosexuals should not be urged to live and behave as heterosexuals against their nature simply because it is more culturally acceptable. For those who argue homosexuality is an orientation, homosexual behavior is not categorically sinful, since such behavior is an expression of a person's created nature. This argument disputes the theological claim that while one's sexual orientation may not be sinful or wrong, their BEHAVIOR may be (thus the slogan, "Love the sinner, hate the sin").

Out – being openly HOMOSEXUAL, BISEXUAL, or TRANSGENDER, i.e., *out* of the CLOSET.

Outing – the intentional or unintentional disclosing of a HOMOSEXUAL, BI-SEXUAL, or TRANSGENDER person's sexual ORIENTATION or GENDER IDENTITY without her or his consent; i.e., forcing someone *out* of the CLOSET.

Pedophilia – adult sexual attraction to prepubescent children; can lead to child molestation. Negative social attitudes about minority groups often manifest in the message that members of the despised group are a threat to children. In HETEROSEXIST culture, HOMOSEXUALS (most often men) have been irrationally and unjustly stereotyped as pedophiles in order to perpetuate HOMOPHOBIA. This misinformation should be countered in the pulpit.

Pink Triangle – originally the mark used to identify homosexual men sent by the Nazis to concentration and work camps along with Jews, gypsies, and Catholic priests. In the twentieth century, the pink triangle symbol was reappropriated by the gay community as a sign of empowerment.

Preference – see CHOICE.

Queen – slur for a flamboyant or effeminate HOMOSEXUAL man (as in DRAG QUEEN) and by extension any gay man. How the term came to be used in this way is unclear and debated. While the term can be used as a HETEROSEXIST insult and thus should never be used in the pulpit, the term is used as acceptable slang by some within the GAY community.

Queer – generally meaning "strange" or "unusual," the term was used as a HOMOPHOBIC slur for HOMOSEXUALS. The term was reappropriated by some HOMOSEXUAL activists in an attempt to move toward liberating themselves from the oppressive power of others' labels. Since the late twentieth century *queer* has been used more broadly by people to identify themselves as sexual minorities while resisting the categories of HETEROSEXUAL, HOMOSEXUAL, BISEXUAL, or TRANSGENDER. Because the term is still used in popular speech as a slur, it should be avoided or only used with careful explanation in the pulpit.

Questioning – (synonym, INQUIRING) term for individuals who are uncertain about and seeking answers concerning their sexual ORIENTATION or GENDER IDENTITY. In the acronym LGBTQI, the Q can be understood to stand either for QUESTIONING or QUEER.

Rainbow Flag – a symbol of LGBTQI pride commonly used in the gay rights movement, representing the great diversity in the movement.

Reparative Therapy – (synonym, CONVERSION THERAPY) psychotherapy aimed at managing clients' HOMOSEXUAL BEHAVIOR through CELIBACY and/or changing her or him to be attracted to persons of the opposite sex. The assumption behind such therapy is that same-sex feelings and actions are either sinful CHOICES or signs of mental illness that when properly treated can be eliminated or managed. While such therapy can be performed in a secular setting (e.g., National Association for Research and Therapy of Homosexuality—NARTH), it is usually practiced by religious organizations (e.g., Exodus International). Since the 1970s, major medical and mental health association have rejected the claim that homosexuality is a psychological disorder, and since the 1990s they have consistently condemned the goals and methods of reparative therapy.

Sex – the biological and physiological characteristics that define males and females. The term is contrasted with GENDER as a technical sociological/anthropological term defining what is feminine or masculine.

Sex Reassignment Surgery – the procedure by which a person's physical appearance and the function of their existing sexual characteristics are altered to resemble that of the other SEX. It is part of a treatment for gender identity disorder/GENDER DYSPHORIA in transexual and transgender people. It may also be performed on INTERSEX people, often in infancy.

Special Rights – a derisive term referring to rights meant to create equal opportunities for minority groups (established for instance in accessibility laws for the disabled, affirmative action, and hate crime punishments) as actually being rights not offered universally. In debate concerning rights for homosexuals, the term is primarily used in contrast to EQUAL RIGHTS. For instance, is the right for a GAY couple to marry an equal right (all have the right to marry) or a special right (all have the right to marry a person of the opposite sex, not the right to marry someone of the same sex)? This concept should be countered in the pulpit.

Straight – slang synonym for HETEROSEXUAL. The derivation of the term is unclear, but it possibly originated with HOMOSEXUAL men in the 1940s who referred to ceasing to have homosexual sex as "going straight" in the sense of "straight and narrow," as a contrast to British slang that referred to being GAY as "bent." While some find the term "straight" problematic in that it implies HETERONORMATIVITY, it is a generally accepted term appropriate for the pulpit.

Transgender – an umbrella term for persons whose GENDER IDENTITY, gender expression, or behavior does not conform to that typically associated with the SEX to which they were assigned at birth. The prefix *trans-* derives from the Latin meaning "across" or "beyond." Included under the umbrella are subcategories such as *transman/transwoman*, CROSS-DRESS, DRAG KING/QUEEN, TRANSVESTITE, and TRANSEXUAL. Transgender identity may be distinct from sexual attraction/ORIENTATION.

Transman/Transwoman – see TRANSEXUAL

Transexual – a TRANSGENDER person who seeks to transition or has transitioned to the other physical SEX through hormone therapy and/or reassignment surgery changing their sexual anatomy to align with their GENDER IDENTITY. A person who transitions from a male physiology to a female physiology and identity is called a *transwoman*. A person who transitions from female physiology to male physiology and identity is called a *transman*.

Transvestite – an outdated term for a TRANSGENDER individual who CROSS-DRESSES. The term was coined in the early twentieth century and derives from the Latin *trans-*, meaning "across," and *vestitus*, "dressed".

www.ingramcontent.com/pod-product-compliance
Lightning Source LLC
Chambersburg PA
CBHW020333100426
42812CB00029B/3111/J